Fatal Charms

ALSO BY DOMINICK DUNNE

The Winners
The Two Mrs. Grenvilles

Fatal Charms

and Other Tales of Today

Dominick Dunne

Crown Publishers, Inc.
New York

Published by Crown Publishers, Inc. 225 Park Avenue South, New York 10003 and represented in Canada by the Canadian MANDA Group.

CROWN is a trademark of Crown Publishers, Inc.

Manufactured in the United States of America

Book design by Dana Sloan

Library of Congress Cataloging-in-Publication Data

Dunne, Dominick.

    Fatal charms and other tales of today.

    I. Title.

PS3554.U492F3   1987   814'.54   86-16834

ISBN 0-517-56452-1

10 9 8 7 6 5 4

For E.G.D. with love

Contents

A Word on a Late Start

Several years ago, when breaking up a house I had lived in for years in California, I came across a long-forgotten box of letters from World War II which I, as a young soldier of eighteen and nineteen, wrote to my mother, father, and sisters from several combat zones in the European theater of operations. In the same box were letters that my family had written to me in return that I must have carried around in my pack and saved. Reading what I wrote to my family, and what my family wrote back to me, after thirty-five years was an eerie experience: an almost day-by-day account of their life in Hartford, Connecticut, during wartime concurrent with mine as a teenage private in France, Belgium, and Germany in 1944 and 1945. More startling than our separate histories, however, was the revision of a resentment I had long nurtured about my late father. For years I believed he had considered me to be a disappointment as a son because my interests were always more artistic than athletic. To my astonishment his letters were filled not with the stern admonishments which were my memory of him but with pride that I was fighting for my country, admiration for my descriptions of the events of war, and some long-term advice that I should give some thought, after completing college, to a career in writing.

I didn't take his advice. My father died before I finished Williams College, and my life choices were my own to make. I had been bitten by the theater bug at Williams and decided on a career in television in New York during that early period of live drama that has subsequently become known as the

Golden Age. Then came Hollywood where I spent twenty-four years in television and movies as both a producer and studio executive, and began a long fascination not only with the film industry but also with the social life of the industry, where so many of the business decisions had their genesis.

Within me lurked some sort of documentarian's need to record the extraordinary insider's life that became available to me. For nearly a decade I kept copious scrapbooks and photograph albums with the intensity of someone who knew that none of it was going to last, at least for the recorder of the events. In these books are pictures of my serene and beautiful wife and our children staring out from a variety of exotic settings, and invitations to and photographs of party after party after party. There is a photograph of Natalie Wood applying lipstick, using the blade of a dinner party knife as a mirror; there is Cecil Beaton using a spoon to eat the ice cream from an ice-cream cone; there is Warren Beatty playing the piano in black tie at a Vincente Minnelli party; there is Truman Capote in a deep dancing dip with Tuesday Weld; there is a married acting couple called Nancy Davis and Ronald Reagan who, even then, before politics, were gazing fondly at each other.

In 1978 I repaired to a small cabin in the Cascade Mountains of Oregon to lick the wounds of defeat in Hollywood. My once glamorous life in that community had gone awry, and the pain of a failed marriage that I was not able to let go of, and a failed career that had let go of me, had led me to self-destructive excesses. It was there in the cabin on the Metolius River near a community called Camp Sherman that I finally took up my father's wartime advice and began writing a novel. The process of writing was not unknown to me. In my previous career I always worked closely with writers and, long before I began to write, I often read the in-progress work of my writer friends and felt creative stirrings. An inner contentment that had long eluded me began to come back in Oregon, and I gave serious thought to remaining permanently in that sylvan glade.

Then two things happened. I received a surprising letter from Truman Capote, another dabbler in self-destructive excesses. A longtime acquaintance, although never a friend, he had several times been a guest at our house in Beverly Hills during the jubilant days of my marriage. His was a letter of encouragement and admiration that I had dropped out of my life in order to try to pull it together again. Perhaps he knew it was what he should have done himself. "But remember this," he wrote, "that is not where you belong, and when you get out of it what you went there to get, you have to come back to your own life." Shortly thereafter one of my brothers committed suicide, and I flew east from Oregon to attend his funeral. It was then that I realized it was time for me to begin another chapter.

I returned to Beverly Hills just long enough to sell every possession I once thought I could never live without—pictures, furniture, even all my books—and with two suitcases and a typewriter moved to a little apartment in Greenwich Village to start a new life and a new career. I finished the book I began in Oregon, and it was published with not only no stir but also with a lousy review in the *New York Times.* However, I was thrilled that at past fifty I was published at all and even reviewed in the *Times,* no matter how badly, and, undeterred, I set about writing a new novel that eventually became *The Two Mrs. Grenvilles.*

At five o'clock in the morning on October 31, 1982, I received a call in my New York apartment from a detective in Beverly Hills to tell me that my youngest child and only daughter, Dominique, had been brutally attacked by a former boyfriend of hers and taken to Cedars-Sinai Hospital in Los Angeles. My wife, Lenny, with whom I had remained friendly after the divorce, got on the telephone after the detective. Suffering now from multiple sclerosis and confined to a wheelchair, she filled me in on the terrible details. When I hung up, I knew from her that there was no hope for our daughter. My sons and I left for Los Angeles immediately and, for over a year, until after the trial of John Sweeney for the murder of my daughter, the lives of all of us simply stopped.

One night in New York a week or so before I was to return to Los Angeles for the beginning of the trial, I attended a small dinner party at the home of the writer Marie Brenner. Sitting next to me was a young and attractive Englishwoman by the name of Tina Brown, who had been described to me by Marie as the person who had single-handedly saved the *Tatler*, an English magazine which I was then familiar with only by name. Tina had been brought to New York by Condé Nast to give assistance to the editors of the revised *Vanity Fair*, a magazine experiencing birth pangs in its reincarnation and the object of derisive stories and jokes about its almost certain demise. We liked each other that night and got on well together. She told me I shouldn't waste my Hollywood anecdotes at dinner parties but should write about them. A day or so before I left for Los Angeles, we had lunch together, and there began a professional association between us that has been a profound one in my life. I had never attended a trial until the trial of the man who murdered my daughter, and the charade that called itself justice appalled and disgusted me. Because of Tina, because I trusted her, I wrote the piece called "Justice" that opens this book. By the time that article appeared, in March 1984, Tina had become the editor of *Vanity Fair*, and the salvage job she did in London on the *Tatler* she repeated in New York on *Vanity Fair*, giving the magazine the identity it had heretofore lacked.

The association with Tina Brown has been an intimate one professionally. Sometimes the ideas for articles are hers, sometimes mine. Sometimes they don't work. Occasionally she has been disappointed and more than once has chosen not to publish a story I had traveled afar to research and write. But that's the magazine business. I've covered several trials, most notably the second trial of Claus von Bülow for the attempted murder of his heiress wife Sunny, and I've interviewed a lot of interesting people.

Many of the stories you will read here are ongoing, with

their third acts yet to be played. Claus von Bülow, since his acquittal, continues to live in Sunny's Fifth Avenue apartment with his mistress, Andrea Reynolds. He travels to London for society balls, but his celebrity in New York has abated. It is a curious comment on our time that, convicted and facing thirty years, Claus von Bülow was more of a social draw than he has been since his acquittal. Despite his protests of wanting to work, von Bülow remains a gentleman of leisure while Mrs. Reynolds is the more industrious, having received, according to Liz Smith, the columnist, a publishing advance of $1 million to write her account of her life with Claus during his tribulations. A popular story in New York society is that when von Bülow was asked if he intended to help Andrea Reynolds on her book, he replied, with his famous mordant humor, "No, no, I don't know anything about commas. I only know about comas."

Elsewhere, Candy Spelling is still building her palace with its indoor ice-skating rink. Muriel Slatkin is still suing Ivan Boesky, husband of her sister Seema, for misappropriation of Beverly Hills Hotel funds. Imelda Marcos is still living in reduced circumstances in Honolulu. Elizabeth Taylor is still slender, still sober, and still getting her name in the papers every day. Ava Gardner is still seeking anonymity in London and getting it. Mortimer's is still packing them in, although Claus von Bülow is rarely seen there any more. Gloria Vanderbilt has finished another volume of her autobiography; and the ladies of Palm Beach, even as we speak, are probably getting ready for another party.

John Sweeney, the murderer of my daughter, was released from prison on June 21, 1986, after serving three years. His six-year sentence was automatically reduced to three, less the time he had already served in jail waiting for trial, plus an additional six months for attempting to strangle Dominique a few weeks before he succeeded in strangling her. His lawyer, Michael Adelson, never one to miss an opportunity for self-promotion, reported to the *Santa Monica Evening Outlook,* on the day of his client's release, that Sweeney had been a model prisoner. Adelson further went on to say that Sweeney carries a pocket Bible with him at all times.

Looking over these pieces, it strikes me that they may have something interesting to say of charms fatal and benign, of justice received and justice denied.

Fatal
Charms

Justice:
A Father's Account of
the Trial of His
Daughter's Killer

IT WAS THE beginning of a long hot summer. I flew to Los Angeles on July 5, 1983, for an indefinite stay. Throughout the flight from New York I engaged in diligent conversation with the stranger next to me, postponing as long as possible facing the feelings of dread within me. My two sons, Griffin and Alex, had preceded me out from New York. Alex, the younger one, met me at the airport, and we drove into Beverly Hills to the house where my former wife, Ellen Griffin Dunne, called Lenny, lives. Griffin was already there. It is not the house we lived in as a family. It is smaller and on one level. Lenny has multiple sclerosis and is confined to a wheelchair. We were gathering, a family again, for a murder trial.

The first time I saw Lenny she was getting off a train at the railroad station in Hartford, Connecticut. She was ravishing, and I knew that instant that I would marry her if she would have me. We had a large wedding at her family's ranch in Nogales, Arizona, in 1954, and after living briefly in New York, we moved to Beverly Hills, where I worked for twenty-five years in television and films. We had five children, two of whom died when they were only a few days old. Long divorced, we have, rightly or wrongly, never become unmarried. Often I have felt through the years that our lives might have been better if we had just stuck out the difficult years of our marriage, but I do not know if she would agree with that. We never venture into the realm of what might have been. I refer to her in conversation as my wife, never my ex-wife, and there is not a day in which she does not occupy my thoughts for some period of time. We communicate regularly and mail each other clippings we cut out of newspapers, and I no longer resent, as I once did, addressing her as Mrs. E. Griffin Dunne rather than as Mrs. Dominick Dunne.

When the telephone in my New York apartment woke me at five o'clock in the morning on October 31, 1982, I sensed as I reached for the receiver that disaster loomed. Det. Harold Johnston of the Los Angeles Homicide Bureau told me that my twenty-two-year-old daughter, Dominique, was near death at Cedars-Sinai Medical Center. I asked him if he had notified my wife. He said he was calling from her home. Lenny got on the phone and said, "I need you."

"What happened?" I asked, afraid to hear.

"Sweeney," she answered.

"I'll be on the first plane."

I called Griffin, then twenty-seven, who lives two blocks away from me in New York, and within minutes he was at my door. He called TWA and reserved a seat on the next flight. Then he went to an automatic teller machine and got me money. As I threw clothes into a suitcase, I hesitated over my black suit and tie, thinking they might be bad luck, but I packed them. Before I got into the taxi, I hugged Griffin and kissed him. He was to go then to the apartment of my second son, Alex, and break the news to him. Uniquely individual, Alex chose to live with no telephone on Pitt Street in a relatively inaccessible part of New York. Only Alex, of the four of us, had voiced his dislike of John Sweeney when Dominique introduced him into our lives.

She had brought him to New York several months earlier for the boys and me to meet. Dominique was a successful young television actress, who had just made her first major feature film, *Poltergeist.* Sweeney was the head chef at Ma Maison, a West Hollywood restaurant so concerned with its fashionable image that it had an unlisted telephone number to discourage the *hoi polloi* from entering its portals. We watched an episode of the television series "Fame" in which Dominique was the guest star, and then went out to dinner. At one moment when the four of us were alone, the boys teased Dominique about marriage, and she said, oh no, she was not getting married, and I knew she meant it. I was relieved, for although I could see Sweeney was excessively devoted to her, there was something off-putting about him. That night I phoned her mother and said, "He is much more in love with her than she is with him," and Lenny said, "You're absolutely right."

The next morning Alex told me of an incident that had occurred in P.J. Clarke's after I left them. While Sweeney was in the men's room, a man at the bar recognized Dominique as the older sister in *Poltergeist* and called out one of her lines from the film: "What's happening?" Dominique screams that line when evil spirits start to take over her home and cause frightening things to happen. A film clip of that scene has been shown so often on television that the line was familiar to people all over the country. There was no flirtation; it was the case of a slightly tipsy fan delighted to be in the presence of an actress he had seen in a film. But when Sweeney returned to the table and saw the man talking to Dominique, he became enraged. He picked up the man and shook him. Alex said that Sweeney's reaction was out of all proportion to the innocent scene going on. Alex said he was scary.

The following day I arrived a few minutes late at Lutèce, where I was meeting Dominique and Sweeney for lunch. They had not yet arrived, so I sat at a table in the bar to wait for them. I finished one Perrier and ordered another, and was beginning to think there had been a misunderstanding about either the time or the place when they entered the restaurant. It was a hot summer day, and Dominique looked marvelous in a starched white organdy dress, very California-looking. I was immediately aware that she had been crying, and that there was tension between them.

The chef made a great fuss over Sweeney. There was kissing on both cheeks, and they spoke together in French. At the chef's suggestion we ate the *specialité* of the day, whatever it was, but the lunch was not a success. I found Sweeney ill at ease, nervous, difficult to talk to. It occurred to me that Dominique might have difficulty extricating herself from such a person, but I did not pursue the thought.

On the Fourth of July the three of us dined at the River Café under the Brooklyn Bridge. It was a lovely night, and we were at a window table where we could watch the fireworks. Sweeney told me he intended to leave Ma Maison. He said he had backing from a consortium of French and Japanese businessmen and was going to open his own restaurant on Melrose Park, a highly desirable location in Los Angeles. Never once did he speak affectionately of his employer, Patrick Terrail, a member of the French restaurant family that owns the Tour d'Argent in Paris. In fact, I suspected there were bad feelings between them.

On that endless flight to Los Angeles I did not allow myself to consider the possibility of her death. She was making a pilot at Warner Bros. for an NBC miniseries called "V," and I remember thinking that they would have to shoot around her until she was on her feet again. Five weeks earlier she had broken up with John Sweeney, and he had moved out of the house they shared in West Hollywood. Her explanation to me at the time was, "He's not in love with me, Dad. He's obsessed with me. It's driving me crazy."

Two other daughters preceding Dominique died in infancy from a lung disease once common in cesarean births known as hyaline membrane disease. Dominique was all three daughters in one to us, triply loved. She adored her older brothers and was always totally at ease in a sophisticated world without being sophisticated herself. She was a collector of stray animals; in her menagerie were a cat with a lobotomy and a large dog with stunted legs. She went to Westlake School in Los Angeles, then to Taft School in Connecticut, then to Fountain Valley School in Colorado. After that she spent a year in Florence, where she learned to speak Italian. Twice she and I took trips in Italy together. Extravagantly emotional, she was heartbroken when Lenny gave up the family home on Walden Drive because her worsening condition made it unmanageable. I was not surprised when Dominique announced her intention to become an actress. Griffin, who is an actor and a producer, later said jokingly that one day she decided to become an actress and the next week she was on a back lot making a movie, and that from then on she never stopped. It was very nearly true. She loved being an actress and was passionate about her career.

By the time I arrived in Los Angeles at noon that Sunday, the report that Dominique had been strangled outside her home by her former boyfriend and was in a coma at Cedars-Sinai Medical Center was on all the news channels and stations. Mart Crowley, the author of *The Boys in the Band*, the film version of which I had produced, met me at the airport and filled me in with what little information he had got from Lenny. Lenny's house on Crescent Drive was full of people when we got there. (It would stay that way from early morning until late at night for the next seven or eight days, during which relay teams of friends manned the telephones, screened the calls, handled the coffee detail, accepted the endless deliveries of flowers, made all the arrangements for our day-to-day living.) All the television sets and radios were on for news bulletins. In the midst of this confusion sat Lenny in her wheelchair. She was very calm. "The news is not good," she said to me. And within minutes I heard the words "brain damage" being whispered around the house.

Lenny's mother, who had heard the news on the radio, was
on her way from San Diego. Griffin and Alex's plane would
be in in a few hours. My relatives in Hartford called, and, as
the news spread, so did friends in New York and London. A
doctor at the hospital telephoned for my permission to insert
a bolt into Dominique's skull to relieve the pressure on her
brain. Was it absolutely necessary, I asked. Yes, he replied.
All right, I said. I asked him when we could go and see her.
Not yet, he said.

The boys arrived, ashen-faced. When the time came to go
to the hospital, we were full of dreadful apprehension. Some
friends said to Lenny, "You mustn't go. It would be a terrible
mistake to look at her this way. You must remember her as
she was." They were, of course, thinking of Lenny's health;
stress is the worst thing for multiple sclerosis victims. She
replied, "The mistake would be if I didn't see her. That is
what I would have to live with."

The four of us proceeded in silence through the maze of
corridors leading to the intensive care unit on the fifth floor
of Cedars-Sinai. One of us, I don't remember which, pushed
Lenny's wheelchair, and the other two flanked her—a for-
mation we would automatically fall into many times in the
year that followed. Outside the double doors of the unit are
printed instructions telling you to buzz and announce yourself.
I did so: "The family of Dominique Dunne is here." We were
told to wait, that someone would come out and get us.

Several people were standing there, among them the actor
George Hamilton. We exchanged greetings. George said his
brother was also in the ICU, and that he had been there the
night before when Dominique was brought in. Another man
introduced himself to us as Ken Johnson, the director of the
pilot Dominique was working on. Waiting nearby was a young
actor in the same film named David Packer, his eyes red from
crying. Packer, we learned, had been in Dominique's house
at the time of the attack and had called the police, albeit too
late. Later we also learned that Packer became so frightened
by the struggle he heard outside on the lawn that he left a

message on a friend's answering machine saying, "If I die tonight, it was by John Sweeney."

A nurse appeared and told us that after we had seen Dominique the doctors would want to talk with us. She said that no one but immediate family would be allowed in, and asked us to show identification. They were afraid the press would try to pass themselves off as members of the family. She warned us that it would be a shock to look at her, that we should be prepared.

I worried about Lenny and looked over at her. She closed her eyes, bowed her head, and took a deep breath. I watched her will strength into herself, through some inner spiritual force, in a moment so intensely private that I dared not, even later, question her about it. Of the four of us, she was the strongest when we entered the room.

At first I did not realize that the person on the bed was Dominique. There were tubes in her everywhere, and the life-support system caused her to breathe in and out with a grotesque jerking movement that seemed a parody of life. Her eyes were open, massively enlarged, staring sightlessly up at the ceiling. Her beautiful hair had been shaved off. A large bolt had been screwed into her skull to relieve the pressure on her brain. Her neck was purpled and swollen; vividly visible on it were the marks of the massive hands of the man who had strangled her. It was nearly impossible to look at her, but also impossible to look away.

Lenny wheeled her chair to the bed, took Dominique's hand in hers, and spoke to her in a voice of complete calm. "Hello, my darling, it's Mom. We're all here, Dominique. Dad and Griffin and Alex. We love you."

Her words released us, and the boys and I stepped forward and surrounded the bed, each touching a different part of Dominique. The nurses had said that she could not hear us, but we felt she could, and took turns talking to her. We prayed for her to live even though we knew that it would be best for her to die.

There was a small conference room in the ICU where we

met periodically over the next four days to discuss her ebbing life. Dr. Edward Brettholz told us that the brain scan was even, meaning that it showed no life, but that it would be necessary to take three more scans so that, in the trial ahead, the defense could not claim that Cedars-Sinai had removed Dominique from the life-support system too soon. This was the first mention of a trial. In the shocked state in which we were operating, we had not yet started to deal with the fact that a murder had taken place.

On the fourth day Lenny said, quite unexpectedly, to the doctors, "When Dominique dies, we would like her organs donated to the hospital." The boys and I knew that was exactly what Dominique would have wanted, but it would not have occurred to us to say so at that moment. Lenny, ill herself with a disease for which there is no cure, understood. Dr. Gray Elrod, with tears in his eyes, said two patients in the hospital were waiting for kidney transplants. We then went in and said good-bye to Dominique for the last time before they took her off the support system. She was wheeled to surgery for the removal of her kidneys, and transplant operations took place almost immediately. Her heart was sent to a hospital in San Francisco. Then her body was turned over to the coroner for an autopsy.

In the *Los Angeles Times* a day or so after the attack, Patrick Terrail, the owner of Ma Maison, described his chef, John Sweeney, as a "very dependable young man" and said he would obtain the best legal representation for him. He made no comment about Dominique, whom he knew, as he knew us, and throughout the long ordeal that followed he did not call on us or write a letter of condolence. Since it was too early then to deal with the magnitude of my feelings for the killer of my daughter, Patrick Terrail became the interim object of my growing rage.

Obtaining the best legal representation for Sweeney took an economy turn when a public defender, Michael Adelson, was assigned to handle the case. We heard from Detective

Johnston that Adelson was highly acclaimed and doggedly tough. Assisting the public defender, however, was Joseph Shapiro, the legal counsel for Ma Maison and a member of the prestigious law firm of Donovan, Leisure, Newton & Irvine. Although Shapiro's role on the defense team was later played down, he was an ever-present but elusive figure from the night following the murder, when he visited Sweeney in the Beverly Hills jail, right up until the day of the verdict, when he exulted in the courtroom.

At the time of the murder Dominique was consistently identified in the press as the niece of my brother and sister-in-law, John Gregory Dunne and Joan Didion, rather than as the daughter of Lenny and me. At first I was too stunned by the killing for this to matter, but as the days passed, it bothered me. I spoke to Lenny about it one morning in her bedroom. She said, "Oh, what difference does it make?" with such despair in her voice that I felt ashamed to be concerned with such a trivial matter at such a crucial time.

In the room with us was my former mother-in-law, Beatriz Sandoval Griffin Goodwin, the widow of Lenny's father, Thomas Griffin, an Arizona cattle rancher, and of Lenny's stepfather, Ewart Goodwin, an insurance tycoon and rancher. She was a strong, uncompromising woman who has never not stated exactly what was on her mind in any given situation, a trait that has made her respected if not always endearing.

"Listen to what he's saying to you," she said emphatically. "It sounds as if Dominique was an orphan raised by her aunt and uncle." Lenny looked up with a changed expression. *"And,"* added her mother, to underscore the point, "she had two brothers as well."

"You handle it," Lenny said to me. I called the publicist Rupert Allan, a family friend, and explained the situation to him. "It's hurtful to us. It's as if we had not only lost her but been denied parentage as well," I said. "It'll be taken care of," Rupert said, and it was.

• • •

On the morning of November 4, while the autopsy was going on, I went to visit the elderly monsignor at the Church of the Good Shepherd in Beverly Hills to make the arrangements for Dominique's funeral. In years past this church was jokingly referred to as Our Lady of the Cadillacs for the affluence of its parishioners. The housekeeper at the rectory told me the monsignor was in the church saying mass. I waited in the front pew until he finished. Then I went back into the vestry with him and explained my reason for coming. He had read of the murder in the newspapers, and I thought I detected in him a slight hesitation over having the funeral of a murder victim in the Good Shepherd Church. I explained to him that we had once been members of the parish, that Dominique had been christened there by him twenty-two years earlier, and that he had come to our home afterward to the reception. The memory was dim to him, so I persisted. I said that Martin Manulis, the producer, who would be giving the eulogy at the funeral, was Dominique's godfather, but that evoked no remembrance either. I then said that Maria Cooper was Dominique's godmother, and at that he looked up. He remembered Maria well, he said, the beautiful daughter of Rocky and Gary Cooper. He told me he had given Gary Cooper the last rites when he died, and had performed the funeral mass. He said he had always hoped Maria would be a nun but that, alas, she had married a Jewish fella (the pianist Byron Janis). By now the church was a certainty. We discussed the music that I wanted played, and settled on eleven o'clock, Saturday, November 6, for the funeral.

On November 5 we discovered that the monsignor had also booked a wedding at eleven on Saturday morning. The mistake came to light when the groom-to-be read in one of Dominique's obituaries that her funeral was to be at the same time and in the same place as his wedding. He telephoned the church, and the church notified us.

Griffin, Alex, Martin Manulis, and I went to the rectory in the afternoon to try to straighten matters out. We waited endlessly, but the monsignor did not appear. The boys became impatient and began yelling up the stairs of the rectory. Finally a priest with a heavy Flemish accent came down, but he did not seem anxious to get mixed up in an error that was not of his making. When we pointed out to him that pandemonium was likely to occur the following morning unless steps were taken, he cooperated in figuring out a plan. As the wedding people refused to move their marriage up an hour, we agreed to have the funeral an hour later. It was too late to inform the newspapers, so we arranged for twelve ushers to be at the church at 10:30 to tell the people arriving for the funeral to come back an hour later.

"I cannot comprehend how such an error could have been made," I said to the priest.

"It's even worse than you realize, Mr. Dunne," he replied.

"What do you mean?"

"The groom in the wedding is a friend of the man who murdered your daughter."

That night on the news we watched John Sweeney being arraigned for Dominique's murder. He was accompanied by the defense team of Michael Adelson and Joseph Shapiro. As we watched, we all began to feel guilty for not having spoken out our true feelings about Sweeney when there was still time to save Dominique from him. In the days that followed, her friends began to tell us how terrified she was of him during the last weeks of her life. I found out for the first time that five weeks previously he had assaulted her and choked her, and that she had escaped from him and broken off her relationship with him. Fred Leopold, a family friend and the former mayor of Beverly Hills, told us during a condolence call that he had heard from a secretary in his law office that John Sweeney had severely beaten another woman a year or so earlier. We passed on this information to Det. Harold Johnston, who stayed close to our family during those days.

Later that night, the eve of the funeral, Dominique appeared on two television programs that had been previously scheduled. Also on television that night was a film I had produced, never before seen on television, and another film my brother had written, also being shown for the first time. We did not watch any of them.

The day of the funeral, November 6, was incredibly hot. Riding the few blocks from Lenny's house on Crescent Drive to the Good Shepherd Church at Santa Monica Boulevard and Bedford Drive, I noticed that the tinsel Christmas decorations were going up on the lampposts of Beverly Hills. As the limousine pulled up in front of the church, I was deeply touched to see Dr. Brettholz from Cedars-Sinai in the crowd arriving for the service. Lenny, her mother, Griffin, Alex, and I were in the first car. When the chauffeur opened the door for us to get out, a hot gust of wind blew multicolored wedding confetti into the car.

The boys helped their grandmother out, and then we got the wheelchair out of the trunk and moved Lenny from the car into the chair.

"There's the mother," we heard someone say, and a phalanx of photographers and television cameramen descended on us, coming within a foot of Lenny's face. Because there were so many steps in the front of the church, we decided to take the wheelchair around to the back, where there was a ramp entrance for handicapped people. The cameramen and photographers walked backward in front of us, shooting film. "No matter what they do, don't say anything," I said to the boys.

Lenny has extraordinary dignity. Dressed curiously for a funeral in a long lavender dress with pearls and a large straw hat, she made no attempt to turn away from the television cameramen. They seemed to respect her, and one by one they dropped away.

The church was filled to capacity, not with curiosity seekers attracted by the sensationalism of Dominique's death, but with people who knew her and loved her. During the service the boys read a poem by Yeats, and Martin Manulis, who had brought me to California twenty-six years earlier to work for him on "Playhouse 90," delivered the eulogy. "Every year of her life," he said, "we spent Christmas Eve together at a carol sing at our house. When she could barely talk, she stood between her brothers and sang what resembled 'O Little Town of Bethlehem' and spoke a single line from the Gospel of Saint Luke, taught to her by her doting parents: 'Because there is no room at the inn.' And standing there with those huge grave eyes, she was, in life, an infanta by Goya, only more beautiful."

A few nights after the funeral, Lenny and I sat in her bedroom, she in her bed, I on it, and watched Dominique in "Hill Street Blues." The episode had been dedicated to her on the air by the producers. We did not talk. We did not cry. We simply stared at the set. She looked so incredibly young. She played a battered child. What we would not know until the trial was that the marks on her neck were real, from John Sweeney's assault on her five weeks before he killed her.

On my first day back in New York after the funeral, I was mugged leaving the subway at twelve noon in Times Square. I thought I was the only person on the stairway I was ascending to the street, but suddenly I was grabbed from behind and pulled off balance. I heard the sound of a switchblade opening, and a hand—which was all I ever saw of my assailant—reached around and held the knife in front of my face. From out of my mouth came a sound of rage that I did not know I was capable of making. It was more animal than human, and I was later told it had been heard a block away. Within seconds people came running from every direction. In his panic my assailant superficially slashed my chin with the blade of his knife, but I had beaten him. I had both my wallet and my life, and I realized that, uncourageous as I am about physical combat, I would have fought before giving in. Whoever that nameless, faceless man was, to me he was John Sweeney.

If Dominique had been killed in an automobile accident, horrible as that would have been, at least it would have been over, and mourning could have begun. A murder is an ongoing event until the day of sentencing, and mourning has to be postponed. After several trips west for preliminary hearings, I returned to Los Angeles in July for the trial.

For a while I drove Dominique's electric blue, convertible Volkswagen. It had stood unused in the driveway of Lenny's house since the murder, a reminder of her that we neither wanted to look at nor could bear to get rid of. I felt strange in the car; too old by far to be driving it, I could always imagine her in it, young and pretty, driving too fast, her beautiful long hair streaming out behind her. In the glove compartment I found a pair of her sunglasses, the ones she called her Annie Hall glasses. I had bought them for her in Florence when I visited her in school there. I took them out of the glove compartment and put them in my briefcase. Throughout the trial, when the going got rough, I would hold them in my hand, or touch them in the inside pocket of my jacket next to my heart, as if I could derive strength from her through them.

Alex was living on Crescent Drive with Lenny. Griffin and his girlfriend, the actress Brooke Adams, had rented a house in Malibu. I was staying at my old friend Tom McDermott's house in Holmsby Hills. On the Saturday afternoon before the Monday morning when the jury selection was to start, Lenny rounded us up at her house. She had received a call from a journalist friend of the family, who said he wanted to meet with us to deliver a message from Mike Adelson, the defense attorney representing John Sweeney. We all had curious feelings about the meeting. Why should the lawyer of our daughter's murderer be contacting us through a journalist rather than through the district attorney? At that point in the proceedings our relationship with the district attorney, Steven Barshop, was still very formal. We called him Mr. Barshop, and he called us Mr. and Mrs. Dunne. We did not even have his home telephone number. We decided in advance that no matter what was said to us at the meeting we would listen to the message and make no comment.

The purpose of the journalist's visit was to offer us a plea bargain so that the case would not have to go to trial. He said that Sweeney was full of remorse and was willing to go to prison. Sweeney would plead guilty to a reduced charge of manslaughter and would serve seven and a half years, but he wanted the assault charge, based on his attack on Dominique five weeks before the murder, dropped. The journalist said that Adelson saw the case, not as a crime, but as a tragedy, of "a blue-collar kid who got mixed up in Beverly Hills society and couldn't handle it."

We had been down the plea-bargain road before. Five months earlier, in February, after the preliminary hearing on the assault charge, a plea bargain had been offered to us by Adelson through the district attorney. At that time we had accepted it, feeling that Lenny's health would be endangered by the trial. I had also seen at that hearing what a ruthless player Adelson was in the courtroom. Later, in May, Adelson had reneged on the plea bargain and opened up the whole matter of the trial, which we thought had been put to rest. Now, within two days of the beginning of jury selection, we were being offered, through a third party, another plea bargain, from which the district attorney had simply been excluded. I felt distrustful and manipulated. I despised the fact that we were supposed to be moved that Sweeney was remorseful and "willing" to serve seven and a half years.

Although the journalist was only a messenger in the situation, the meeting became strained as he presented Adelson's viewpoints. Doubts were put in our mind about the ability of Steven Barshop. There was even a suggestion that Dominique was a participant in the crime. Neighbors would be called, we were told, who would testify that fights were commonplace between Dominique and Sweeney. The journalist said that if the two snitches who had come forward were put on the stand, Adelson would "cut them off at the knees." At that time I didn't know what snitches were; they were fellow prisoners who betray confidences of the cell for lessened sentences. (One prisoner reported that Sweeney had confessed to him that he thought he had the police believing he had

not intended to kill Dominique, and another said that Sweeney had told him that Dominique was a snob, too ambitious,
who deserved what she got.)

The journalist talked a great deal about a lawyer called Paul
Fitzgerald. In the months ahead I was never to meet Fitzgerald, but he was often presented in conversation as a sage of
the court system, with detractors as vocal as his admirers. A
former public defender, Fitzgerald was occasionally appointed
as a conflict lawyer by Judge Burton S. Katz, in whose courtroom the case was being tried. A rumor persisted after the
trial that he wrote Judge Katz's astonishing reversal speech on
the day of the sentencing. He was also a close friend of Michael Adelson's. On that Saturday afternoon, before the jury
selection had begun, Paul Fitzgerald was identified as the
source of the information, reiterated again and again by the
journalist who visited us, that Mike Adelson was a wonderful
man.

It had not been my personal experience to find Mike Adelson a wonderful man. Twice during the February preliminary
hearing he had addressed me in the corridor outside the courtroom as Mr. Sweeney, as if mistaking me for the father of the
killer rather than the father of the victim. A seasoned courtroom observer suggested to me that since I was a sympathetic
figure in the courtroom, it had been Adelson's intention, by
this obvious error, to incite me to make some kind of slur on
him in public. During that same hearing, a young friend of
Dominique's named Bryan Cook recounted a night on the
town with his girlfriend, Denise Dennehy, and Dominique
and Sweeney during which several bottles of champagne were
consumed. Singling Dominique out from the quartet of cele-
brants, Adelson, in questioning Cook, asked several times,
"When Miss Dunne got in from the bars, how drunk was
she?" The obvious intent of this ugly repetition was to give
the impression in the courtroom that my actress daughter was
an out-on-the-town drunkard. No amount of laudatory comment, after those preliminary hearings, would ever convince
me that Mike Adelson was a wonderful man. Mustached and

extremely short, his head topped with a full toupee, Adelson made me think of an angry, miniature bulldog.

The journalist's mission, though instigated with good intentions, only engendered bad feelings.

At nine o'clock on Monday morning, July 11, we gathered in Steven Barshop's office in the Santa Monica Courthouse. Alternately tough-talking and professional, the district attorney is about forty. He achieved public recognition for his prosecution of the killers of Sarai Ribicoff, the journalist niece of Senator Abraham Ribicoff. We felt lucky that Barshop had been assigned to our case by Robert Philibosian, the district attorney of Los Angeles County, but we felt that he did not want any personal involvement with us. Although never discourteous, he was brusque, and he made it very clear that he was running the show and would not tolerate any interference.

Barshop was angered when we told him that a plea bargain had been offered to us by Adelson through a journalist. "You didn't accept it, did you?" he asked. We said we had not. "The matter is out of your hands," he said. "The state wishes to proceed with this trial."

That day he gave us his home phone number, and for the first time we called each other by our first names.

The cast of characters was gathering. Down the corridor from the district attorney's office, several hundred potential jurors were milling about, waiting to be called for examination. Observing the scene from benches along the wall was a group known as the courthouse groupies, old people from Santa Monica who come to the courthouse every day to watch the murder trials. They know all the judges, all the lawyers, all the cases, and all the gossip. An old man in a blue polka-dot shirt and a baseball hat with "Hawaii" on it announced to the group that he was waiting to see Sweeney.

"Who's Sweeney?" asked an old woman with jet black, tightly permed hair.

"The guy who killed the movie star," he answered.

"What movie star?"

"Dominique somebody."

"Never heard of her."

I asked a middle-aged woman in black slacks and a tan blouse who was carrying a small red suitcase and peering in the windows of the doors to Courtroom D where everyone was. She said they had broken for lunch. I asked what time they would be back, and she said at two o'clock. I thanked her. My son Alex told me the woman was Sweeney's mother, who had just arrived after a two-day bus trip from Hazelton, Pennsylvania. I had not thought of Sweeney in terms of family, although I knew he had divorced parents and was the oldest of six children, and that his mother had been a battered wife. It was a well-known fact among the people who knew John Sweeney that he had long since put distance between himself and his family. Alex said that he had been sitting next to Mrs. Sweeney in the courtroom earlier, not knowing who she was, when Joseph Shapiro came over to her, addressed her by name, and said that he disliked being the one to give her the message, but her son did not wish to see her. Alex said her eyes filled with tears. For the next seven weeks we sat across the aisle from her every day, and though we never spoke, we felt compassion for her and knew that she in turn felt compassion for us in the dreadful situation that interlocked our families.

The jury selection took two weeks. Each side could eliminate, by way of peremptory challenge, twenty-six people from the main jury before arriving at the twelve, and six from the alternate jury before arriving at the six. People who had had violent crimes in their families were automatically excused. Women activists and people of obvious intelligence who asked pertinent questions were eliminated by the defense. "What I'm looking for are twelve fascists, and Adelson's looking for twelve bleeding-heart liberals or weirdos, and we'll arrive somewhere in between," said Steven Barshop to me at one point. Adelson had announced that his defense would be based mostly on psychiatric findings. A writer-photographer who was being questioned said he would not accept the testimony of psychiatrists and psychologists as fact. He further said he found defense attorneys manipulative, to which Adelson replied, "Suppose you don't like the way I comb my hair. Would that affect the way you listen to the testimony?" I found this an extraordinary image for a lawyer who wore a toupee to use, and then I realized that he must think that we thought that the quarter pound of hair taped to the top of his head was real. This would help me later to understand the total conviction with which he presented his client's version of the events surrounding the murder, which he knew to be untrue.

Presiding over the case was Judge Burton S. Katz. In his forties, Judge Katz gives the impression of a man greatly pleased with his good looks. He is expensively barbered, deeply tanned, and noticeably dressed in a manner associated more with Hollywood agents than with superior court judges. He has tinted aviator glasses, and on the first day he was wearing designer jeans, glossy white loafers, and no necktie beneath his judicial robes. Every seat in the courtroom was filled, and Judge Katz seemed to like playing to an audience. His explanations to the prospective jurors were concise and clear, and he made himself pleasing to them. He said funny things to make them laugh, but then was careful to warn them against levity.

The completed jury consisted of nine men and three women. The man who became the foreman ran a string of bowling alleys. One of the men was a postman, another a butcher. One worked for an airline and another for a computer company. One was a teacher. One had a juvenile delinquent son serving on a work team. Two of the men were black. One of the women was an Irish Catholic widow with six children, including a twenty-two-year-old daughter. Although we had hoped for more women, we were pleased with the makeup of the jury. On the instructions of the judge, not so much as a nod was ever exchanged between us, not even when we lunched in the same restaurant or met in the lava-

tory. However, I felt I grew to know them as the weeks
passed, even though Steven Barshop often told me, "Don't
ever anticipate a jury. They'll fool you every time."

Judge Katz's relationship with the jury bordered on the
flirtatious, and they responded in kind. If the court was called
for ten, Judge Katz invariably began around eleven, with elab-
orate and charming apologies to the jury. One Monday morning he told them he had had a great weekend in Ensenada,
that he had had the top down on his car both ways, and that
he wished they had been with him. The ladies laughed de-
lightedly, and the men grinned back at him.

Our family was never favored with Judge Katz's charms, not
even to the point of simple courtesies. For seven weeks he
mispronounced Dominique's name, insistently calling her by
my name, Dominick. People wandered in and out of the
courtroom; lawyers from other cases chatted with the clerk or
used the bailiff's telephone. The microphone on the witness
stand fell off its moorings innumerable times and either went
dead or emitted a loud electronic screech, and it was never
fixed.

It is the fashion among the criminal fraternity to find God,
and Sweeney, the killer, was no exception. He arrived daily
in the courtroom clutching a Bible, dressed in black, looking
like a sacristan. The Bible was a prop; Sweeney never read it,
he just rested his folded hands on it. He also wept regularly.
One day the court had to be recessed because he claimed the
other prisoners had been harassing him before he entered,
and he needed time to cry in private. I could not believe that
jurors would buy such a performance. "You mark my words,"
said Steven Barshop, watching him. "Something weird is
going to happen in this trial. I can feel it."

On July 20, Barshop called us to say that Adelson did not
want Lenny at the trial because her presence in a wheelchair
would create undue sympathy for her that would be prejudicial
to Sweeney. She was to appear in court the following day so

that the judge could hear what she had to say and decide if it was relevant to the trial.

We began to worry. It was becoming apparent that nearly everything Adelson requested was being granted. Adelson recognized Katz's enormous appetite for flattery and indulged it shamelessly. A camaraderie sprang up between the judge and the public defender, and the diminutive Adelson made himself a willing participant in a running series of "short" jokes indulged in by the judge at his expense to the delight of the jury. It was becoming equally apparent that the district attorney, Steven Barshop, was ill-favored by the judge.

Lenny did not take the stand the following day. She was preceded by Lillian Pierce, who had been a girlfriend of John Sweeney's before my daughter. Det. Harold Johnston had tracked her down after receiving a telephone tip from Lynne Brennan, a Beverly Hills publicist, who had once been her friend and knew her story. Lillian Pierce appeared by subpoena issued by the prosecution and was known in advance to be a reluctant witness. Later we heard that she had sat in a car outside the church at Dominique's funeral and cried, feeling too guilty to go inside. At Adelson's request, her testimony was given out of the presence of the jury in order to determine its admissibility as evidence.

An attractive and well-dressed woman in her thirties, Lillian Pierce was very nervous and kept glancing over at Sweeney, who did not look at her. She had, she admitted, been in contact the day before with Joseph Shapiro, the Ma Maison lawyer. When the district attorney started to question her, her account of her relationship with John Sweeney was so shocking that it should have put to rest forever the defense stand that the strangulation death of Dominique Dunne at the hands of John Sweeney was an isolated incident. He was, it became perfectly apparent, a classic abuser of women, and his weapon was his hands.

Lillian Pierce said that on ten separate occasions during their two-year relationship he had beaten her. She had been hospitalized twice, once for six days, once for four. Sweeney had broken her nose, punctured her eardrum, collapsed her lung, thrown rocks at her when she tried to escape from him. She had seen him, she said, foam at the mouth when he lost control, and smash furniture and pictures. As she spoke, the courtroom was absolutely silent.

Adelson was incensed by the impact of Lillian Pierce's story, made more chilling by her quiet recital of all the acts of violence that she had survived. He became vicious with her. "Were you not drunk?" he asked her. "Were you not drugged?" His implication was that she had got what she deserved. He tried repeatedly to get her to veer from her story, but she remained steadfast.

"Let me remind you, Miss Pierce," he said testily at one point, shuffling through a sheaf of papers, "when you met with Mr. Joe Shapiro and me for lunch on November third, you said . . ." I stopped following the sentence. My mind remained at the date November 3. On November 3, Dominique was still on the life-support system at Cedars-Sinai. She was not pronounced legally dead until November 4. So even while Dominique lay dying, efforts were being made to free her killer by men who knew very well that this was not his first display of violence. Adelson knew, and sent a journalist to our house with the lachrymose message that he saw Dominique's death not as a crime but as a tragedy. Patrick Terrail had told Detective Johnston that he had seen Sweeney act violently only once, when he "punched out" a telephone booth in the south of France. It is a fact of the legal system that all information gathered by the prosecution relevant to the case is available to the defense. The reverse is not true. If Detective Johnston had not learned about Lillian Pierce from a telephone tip, her existence would have been unknown to us. I felt hatred for Michael Adelson. His object was to win; nothing else mattered.

Steven Barshop cross-examined Lillian Pierce. "Let me ask you, Miss Pierce, do you come from a well-to-do family?"

Adelson objected. "I am trying to establish a pattern," Barshop told the judge.

At that moment—one of the most extraordinary I have ever experienced—we saw an enraged John Sweeney, his prop Bible flying, jump up from his seat at the counsel table and take off for the rear door of the courtroom which leads to the judge's chambers and the holding-cell area. Velma Smith, the court clerk, gave a startled cry. Lillian Pierce, on the stand, did the same. We heard someone shout, "Get help!" Silent alarms were activated by Judge Katz and Velma Smith. The bailiff, Paul Turner, leapt to his feet in a pantherlike movement and made a lunge for Sweeney, grasping him around the chest from behind. Within seconds four armed guards rushed into the courtroom, nearly upsetting Lenny's wheelchair, and surrounded the melee. The bailiff and Sweeney crashed into a file cabinet. "Don't hurt him!" screamed Adelson. Sweeney was wrestled to the floor and then handcuffed to the arms of his chair, where Adelson whispered frantically to him to get hold of himself.

Sobbing, Sweeney apologized to the court and said he had not been trying to escape. Judge Katz accepted his apology. "We know what a strain you are under, Mr. Sweeney," he said. I was appalled at the lack of severity of the judge's admonishment. What we had witnessed had nothing to do with escape. It was an explosion of anger. It showed us how little it took to incite John Sweeney to active rage. Like most of the telling moments of the trial, however, it was not witnessed by the jury.

Mike Tipping, a reporter from the *Santa Monica Evening Outlook*, saw the episode and reported it in his paper. At the behest of Adelson, the court admonished Tipping for exaggerating the incident. The same day, a court gag order was issued to prevent anyone involved in the case from speaking to the press.

From then on, I felt, and continue to feel, that John Sweeney was sedated in the courtroom so that such an incident would never be repeated in front of the jury. He was asked under oath, not in the presence of the jury, if he was sedated, and he said he was not, except for some mild medicine for an upset stomach. The district attorney asked the court for either a blood test or a urine test to substantiate Sweeney's reply, but Judge Katz denied the request.

When Lenny took the stand the first time, the jury was again not present. Judge Katz had to decide on the admissibility of her testimony, but he wrote notes through most of it and scarcely looked in her direction. Lenny described an incident when Dominique came to her house at night after being beaten by Sweeney—the first of the three times he beat her. Dominique's terror was so abject, Lenny said, that she assumed a fetal position in the hallway. Sweeney had knocked her head on the floor and pulled out clumps of her hair. Adelson asked Lenny if she knew what the argument that precipitated the beating had been about. Lenny said she did not. He asked her if she knew that Dominique had had an abortion. She didn't. I didn't. The boys didn't. Her closest friend didn't. It remained throughout the trial an unsubstantiated charge that, to the defense, seemed to justify the beating. The look on Lenny's face was heartbreaking, as if she had been slapped in public. Judge Katz called her testimony hearsay and said he would make his decision as to its admissibility when the trial resumed on August 15 after a two-week hiatus.

During this period, our great friend Katie Manulis died of cancer. Our lives have been intricately involved with the Manuli, as we call them, for twenty-five years. Back at Martin's house after the funeral, I told Sammy Goldwyn that I had grave doubts about the judge. I cited his solicitousness toward Sweeney after his outburst in the courtroom, as well as his discourtesy with Lenny. Sammy said he was dining that evening with John Van de Kamp, the attorney general of the state of California, and he would get a rundown on the judge for me.

He reported back that Judge Katz went to law school at Loyola University and then served as a deputy district attorney for fourteen years. He had been unpopular in the district attorney's office, where he was considered a theatrical character. In 1970, he prosecuted members of the Charles Manson "family" for the murders of Shorty Shea and Gary Hinman. In 1978, he was appointed to the municipal court by Governor Jerry Brown, and in 1981 he was appointed to the superior court. He was considered highly ambitious and was said to like cases with high media visibility, like this one.

Judge Katz ruled that the prosecution could not use the testimony of Lillian Pierce to show the jury that John Sweeney had committed previous acts of violence against women. He said he would allow Miss Pierce to take the stand only in rebuttal if Adelson put expert witnesses, meaning psychiatrists, on the stand to testify that Sweeney was too mentally impaired by emotion to have formed the intent to kill. Once Judge Katz ruled that, Adelson threw out his psychiatric defense. Later in the trial, when the possibility of putting Lillian Pierce on the stand was raised again by Steven Barshop, Katz ruled that the "prejudicial effect outweighed the probative value." The jury would never know of Lillian Pierce's existence until after they had arrived at a verdict.

Judge Katz also ruled that Lenny's testimony about Dominique's coming to her in hysterics after Sweeney first beat her on August 27 could not be used by the prosecution during the main case. The judge once again agreed with Adelson that the prejudicial effect of the testimony outweighed its probative value, and he told Barshop not to mention the incident in his primary case. He said he would decide later in the trial whether her story could be used to rebut a mental-impairment defense for Sweeney.

Judge Katz agreed with Adelson that all statements made by Dominique to her agent, her fellow actors, and her friends regarding her fear of John Sweeney during the last five weeks of her life must be considered hearsay and ruled inadmissible as evidence.

It was not an auspicious opening to the trial. The loss of the Lillian Pierce testimony was a severe blow to Steven Barshop. Our hopes were buoyed by Barshop's opening argument in the case. He began with a description of the participants. Sweeney: twenty-seven, six foot one, 170 pounds. Dominique: twenty-two, five foot one, 112 pounds. He gave a rundown of the charges in the two incidents, the assault on Dominique on September 26 and the murder on the night of October 30. He described how Sweeney had walked out of Ma Maison restaurant at 8:30 that evening and proceeded on foot to the house, where he argued with Dominique and strangled her. He said that Dominique was brain-dead there at the scene of the strangulation, despite the fact that she was kept on the life-support system at Cedars-Sinai until November 4. He said that the coroner would testify that death by strangulation took between four and six minutes. Then he held up a watch with a second hand and said to the jury, "Ladies and gentlemen, I am going to show you how long it took for Dominique Dunne to die." For four minutes the courtroom sat in hushed silence. It was horrifying. I had never allowed myself to think how long she had struggled in his hands, thrashing for her life. A gunshot or a knife stab is over in an instant; a strangulation is an eternity. The only sound during the four minutes came from Michael Adelson and John Sweeney, who whispered together the whole time.

Our daily presence in the courtroom annoyed Adelson throughout the trial. Defense lawyers in general don't like jurors to see the victim's family. Friends of ours had advised us to leave town until the trial was over. The organization known as Parents of Murdered Children advised us to attend every session. "It's the last business of your daughter's life," a father of a young girl stabbed to death by a former boyfriend said to me on the telephone one night. We sat in the front row behind the bailiff's desk in full view of the jury: Lenny in the aisle in her wheelchair, Alex, Griffin and his girlfriend, and I. We were within six feet of John Sweeney. As the weeks crept by, the boys became more and more silent. It seemed to me as if their youth were being stripped away from them.

In the row behind us sat representatives from Parents of Murdered Children; some had been through their trials, others were awaiting theirs. Many of Dominique's friends came on a daily basis; so did friends of ours and friends of the boys. There were also representatives from Women Against Violence Against Women and from Victims for Victims, the group started by Theresa Saldana, an actress who was brutally stabbed a few years ago and survived.

"If any member of the Dunne family cries, cries out, rolls his eyes, exclaims in any way, he will be asked to leave the courtroom," we were told by the judge at the behest of Adelson.

"Your honor, Alex Dunne had tears in his eyes," Adelson called out one day. When Sweeney took the stand, Alex and Griffin changed their seats in order to be in his line of vision. Adelson tried to get them put out of the courtroom for this. We were intimidated but never searched. How easy it would have been to enter with a weapon and eradicate the killer if we had been of that mind. As the last week approached, Alex said one morning, "I can't go back anymore. I can't be there where Sweeney is."

Dominique's friends Bryan Cook and Denise Dennehy flew in from Lake Forest, Illinois, to testify about the time, five weeks before the murder, when Sweeney attempted to choke Dominique after their night on the town. She had escaped from her house that night by climbing through a bathroom window and driving her Volkswagen to the home of an artist friend named Norman Carby. (Lenny was in New York at the time.) Carby, appalled by the marks of attempted strangulation on her neck, had the presence of mind to take photographs. The pictures were the prosecution's prime exhibit of the seriousness of the assault. Adelson belittled the pictures. There was, he said, a third picture in the same series showing

Dominique laughing. Carby explained that Dominique had a reading that morning for the role of a battered child on "Hill Street Blues." Carby said he told her that at least she wouldn't have to wear any makeup for it, and that had made her laugh.

One of the snitches appeared in the courtroom. He was the one who claimed Sweeney had said he thought he had the police believing that he had not intended to kill Dominique. He claimed further that Sweeney had asked him, "Have you ever been with a girl who thought she was better than you?" Snitches are known to be unreliable witnesses, whom jurors usually dislike and distrust. This man's dossier, forwarded by his prison, depicted a disturbed troublemaker. His arms were tattooed from his shoulders to his wrists. Steven Barshop decided to dispense with his revelations. He was not put on the stand.

On one of the color pictures of the autopsy there was a bruise on Dominique's shoulder, which gave rise to disagreement. No one was quite sure if it had been incurred when she fell to the ground after being strangled, or if it had been caused by the life-support system, or if it was a result of the autopsy. Adelson was determined that the jury not see the photograph with the bruise, and the arguments went on endlessly while the jury waited in an adjoining room. Judge Katz solved the matter: with a pair of scissors provided by Velma Smith, the court clerk, he simply cut off the picture below the neck so that only the actual strangulation marks were visible to the jury.

Dep. Frank DeMilio, one of the first to arrive at the scene of the crime, testified on the stand that Sweeney had said to him, "Man, I blew it. I killed her. I didn't think I choked her that hard, but I don't know, I just kept on choking her. I just lost my temper and blew it again."

I wondered then and wonder still what the word *again* meant. Did it refer to one of the other times he attacked Dominique? Or Lillian Pierce? Or is there something else in this mysterious man's mysterious past that has not yet come to light? Sweeney had no car and no driver's license, an oddity for a young man in a city totally dependent on wheels. And although he had worked as head chef in one of the most prestigious restaurants in the city, he was nearly totally without funds. Furthermore, an informant at Ma Maison told Detective Johnston of another former girlfriend, then somewhere in France, against whom Sweeney had committed at least one act of violence.

After Steven Barshop rested his case, Judge Katz delivered another devastating blow to the prosecution. He agreed with a request from Adelson that the jury be allowed to consider only charges of manslaughter and second-degree murder, thus acquitting Sweeney of first-degree murder. In asking Katz to bar a first-degree murder verdict, Adelson argued, "There is no premeditation or deliberation in this case," and Katz agreed. Barshop argued that the jury should decide whether there was sufficient premeditation or deliberation. He said Sweeney had enough time to consider his actions during the period—up to six minutes, according to the coroner's testimony—that it took him to choke Dominique. Katz emphasized that Sweeney had arrived at Dominique's house without a murder weapon, although he knew that Sweeney's hands had nearly killed Lillian Pierce and that his hands had nearly strangled Dominique five weeks before he killed her. He also cited the fact that Sweeney had made no attempt to escape.

Rarely do twelve people on a jury agree: most verdicts are compromises. If this jury had had the option of first-degree murder and were in dispute, they could have compromised at second-degree. With first-degree ruled out, if there was a dispute, their only compromise was manslaughter.

Det. Harold Johnston was in the courtroom that day. He believed this was a case of first-degree murder, just as we did. Means of escape and means of method have nothing to do with premeditation, he told us. An informant at Ma Maison had told us that just before Sweeney left the restaurant to go to Dominique's house on the night he murdered her, he had ordered two martinis from the bar and drunk them. He felt that Sweeney must have decided that if he couldn't have Dominique, he wasn't going to let anyone else have her either.

Harold Johnston had become a friend over the year, since the night that he rang the doorbell of Lenny's house on Crescent Drive at two in the morning to tell her that Dominique was near death in Cedars-Sinai. He had also questioned Sweeney on the night of the murder. He told me in the corridor outside the courtroom that day that the judge's ruling had made him lose faith in the system after twenty-six years on the force.

One day Adelson's wife and little boys came to the trial. As if to offset his unpleasant image in front of the jury, Adelson elaborately played father. "Now don't you talk," he admonished them, wagging his finger. Several times Judge Katz's mother and father also came to observe the proceedings. They were seated in special chairs set up inside the gate by the bailiff's desk and whispered incessantly. Invariably Katz showed off for their benefit. On one occasion, after both Barshop and Adelson had finished with the witness David Packer, the actor who was visiting Dominique at the time of the murder and who called the police, Judge Katz started an independent line of questioning, about eyeglasses, that had not been introduced by either the prosecution or the defense: Did David Packer wear them? Did he have them on the night he saw Sweeney standing over Dominique's body? The questions advanced nothing and muddied what had gone before.

A photographer from *People* magazine appeared in court one day, weighed down with equipment. I happened to know him. He said he had been sent to take pictures of our family for an article his magazine was doing on the trial. Neither

Griffin nor Alex wished to be photographed, but the photographer stayed in the courtroom and took pictures of the session with Sweeney and the lawyers. At the lunch break, the judge signaled to the photographer to see him in his chambers. Later, out in the parking lot, I ran into the man. He told me he had thought the judge was going to ask him not to shoot during the session. Instead, the judge had said he wanted his eyes to show up in the pictures and had tried on several different pairs of glasses for the photographer's approval.

Adelson had never intended to have Sweeney take the stand. However, when he had to throw out his psychiatric defense to keep the jurors from knowing about Sweeney's previous acts of violence against Lillian Pierce, he had no choice but to put the accused on. Sweeney was abjectly courteous, addressing the lawyers and judge as sir. He spoke very quietly, and often had to be told to raise his voice so that the jurors could hear. Although he wept he never once became flustered, and there was no sign of the rage he exhibited on the day Lillian Pierce took the stand. He painted his relationship with Dominique as nearly idyllic. He gave the names of all her animals—the bunny, the kitten, the puppy. He refuted the testimony of Bryan Cook and Denise Dennehy and denied that he had attempted to choke Dominique after their night on the town five weeks before the murder. He said he'd only tried to restrain her from leaving the house. He admitted that they had separated after that, and that she had had the locks changed so that he could not get back in the house, but he insisted that she had promised to reconcile with him and that her refusal to do so was what brought on the final attack. He could not, he claimed, remember the events of the murder, which prompted Barshop to accuse him of having "selective memory." After the attack, Sweeney said, he had entered the house and attempted to commit suicide by swallowing two bottles of pills; however, no bottles were ever found, and if he had swallowed pills, they did not have any apparent effect on his system.

From the beginning we had been warned that the defense would slander Dominique. It is part of the defense premise that the victim is responsible for the crime. As Dr. Willard Gaylin says in his book *The Killing of Bonnie Garland*, Bonnie Garland's killer, Richard Herrin, murdered Bonnie all over again in the courtroom. It is always the murder victim who is placed on trial. John Sweeney, who claimed to love Dominique, and whose defense was that this was a crime of passion, slandered her in court as viciously and cruelly as he had strangled her. It was agonizing for us to listen to him, led on by Adelson, besmirch Dominique's name. His violent past remained sacrosanct and inviolate, but her name was allowed to be trampled upon and kicked, with unsubstantiated charges, by the man who killed her.

"Look at her friends!" I wanted to scream at the judge and the jury. "You have seen them both on the stand and in the courtroom: Bryan Cook, Denise Dennehy, Melinda Bittan, Kit McDonough, Erica Elliot, and the others who have been here every day—bright, clean-cut, successful young people. That is what Dominique Dunne was like. She wasn't at all the person whom John Sweeney is describing." But I sat silent.

When Dominique's friends closed up her house after the funeral, her best friend, Melinda Bittan, came across a letter Dominique had written to Sweeney, which he may or may not have received. The letter had been filed away and forgotten. In the final days of the trial, Melinda remembered it one day when a group of us were having lunch together. Steven Barshop introduced it in his rebuttal, and as the court reporter, Sally Yerger, read it to the jury, it was as if Dominique was speaking from beyond the grave.

"Selfishness works both ways," she wrote. *"You are just as selfish as I am. We have to be two individuals to work as a couple.*

I am not permitted to do enough things on my own. Why must you be a part of everything I do? Why do you want to come to my riding lessons and my acting classes? Why are you jealous of every scene partner I have?

"Why must I recount word for word everything I spoke to Dr. Black about? Why must I talk about every audition when you know it is bad luck for me? Why do we have discussions at 3:00 A.M. all the time, instead of during the day?

"Why must you know the name of every person I come into contact with? You go crazy over my rehearsals. You insist on going to work with me when I have told you it makes me nervous. Your paranoia is overboard. . . . You do not love me. You are obsessed with me. The person you think you love is not me at all. It is someone you have made up in your head. I'm the person who makes you angry, who you fight with sometimes. I think we only fight when images of me fade away and you are faced with the real me. That's why arguments erupt out of nowhere.

"The whole thing has made me realize how scared I am of you, and I don't mean just physically. I'm afraid of the next time you are going to have another mood swing. . . . When we are good, we are great. But when we are bad, we are horrendous. The bad outweighs the good."

Throughout Steven Barshop's closing argument to the jury, when he asked them to find Sweeney guilty of murder in the second degree, the maximum verdict available to them, Judge Katz sat with a bottle of correction fluid, brushing out lines on something he was preparing. Later we learned it was his instructions to the jury. I thought, if he isn't listening, or is only half listening, what kind of subliminal signal is that sending to the jury? During Adelson's final argument, on the other hand, he gave his full attention.

"This will be the toughest day of the trial," said Steven Barshop on the morning of Adelson's final argument. "Today you will hear Adelson justify murder." We had grown very close to Steven Barshop during the weeks of the trial and admired his integrity and honesty. "You don't have to sit through it, you know," he said. But we did, and he knew we would.

I lost count of how many times Adelson described Sweeney to the jury as an "ordinarily reasonable person," as if this act of murder were an isolated instance in an otherwise serene life. Every time he said it he separated the three words— ordinarily reasonable person—and underscored them with a pointing gesture of his hand. We who had seen every moment of the trial knew of thirteen separate instances of violence, ten against Lillian Pierce and three against Dominique, but the jurors at this point were still not even aware of the exis-tence of Lillian Pierce. Through an informant at Ma Maison, our family also knew of other acts of violence against women that had not been introduced into the case, but we sat in impassive silence as Adelson described the strangler as an ordinarily reasonable person.

He returned to his old theme: "This was not a crime," he told the jury. "This was a tragedy." It didn't matter that he knew it wasn't true. They didn't know it wasn't true, and he was concerned only with convincing them.

He talked about "that old-fashioned thing: romantic love." He made up dialogue and put it in the mouth of Dominique Dunne. "I, Dominique, reject you Sweeney," he cried out. "*I lied to you, Sweeney!*"

We were sickened at his shamelessness. Leaving the court-room during a break, I found myself next to him in the aisle. "You piece of shit," I said to him quietly so that only he could hear.

His eyes flashed in anger. "Your Honor!" he called out. "May I approach the bench?"

I continued out to the corridor, where I told Lenny what I had done.

"That was very stupid," she said. "Now you'll get kicked out of the courtroom."

"No one heard me say it except Adelson," I said. "When the judge calls me up, I'll lie and say I didn't say it. Everybody else is lying. Why shouldn't I? It's his word against mine."

Steven Barshop appeared.

"Is he going to kick me out?" I asked.

Barshop smiled. "He can't kick the father of the victim out of the court on the last day of the trial with all the press present," he said. Then he added, "But don't do it again."

Judge Katz drank soft drinks from Styrofoam cups as he read instructions to the jury explaining second-degree murder, voluntary manslaughter, and involuntary manslaughter. Later, after the sentencing, the jury foreman, Paul Spiegel, would say on television that the judge's instructions were incomprehensible. During the eight days that the jury was out, deadlocked, they asked the judge four times for clarification of the instructions, and four times the judge told them that the answers to their questions were in the instructions.

I was now living in the Bel Air home of Martin Manulis, who had returned east after Katie's death to complete postproduction work on a new miniseries. The jury had been out for over a week, and we knew they could not understand the instructions. Lenny, Griffin, Alex, and I were terribly edgy, and one evening we all went our separate ways. I paced restlessly from room to room in the Manulis house. I hadn't looked at television that summer except occasionally to see the news, but I suddenly picked up the remote-control unit and flicked the set on. I froze at the voice I heard.

There, on television, was Dominique screaming. "What's happening?" I had not known that *Poltergeist* was scheduled on the cable channel, and the shock of seeing her was overwhelming. I felt as if she were sending me a message. "I don't know what's happening, my darling," I screamed back at the television set, and for the first time since the trial started, I sobbed. The next day the verdict came in.

The waiting was endless. Joseph Shapiro, the Ma Maison lawyer, regaled the reporters with an account of an African safari in the veldt where the native guides serving his party

wore black tie. One of the courthouse groupies said that three
buzzes to the clerk's desk meant that a verdict had been
reached. Five minutes before the jury entered, we watched
Judge Katz sentence a man who had robbed a flower shop in
a nonviolent crime to five years in prison. Sweeney entered,
clutching his Bible, and sat a few feet away from us. Mrs.
Sweeney sat across the aisle with Joseph Shapiro. The room
was packed. A pool television camera, reporters, and photographers filled the aisles.

The jury entered, and the foreman, Paul Spiegel, delivered
two envelopes to the bailiff to give to the judge. Katz opened
first one envelope and then the other, milking his moment
before the television camera like a starlet at the Golden
Globes. Then, revealing nothing, he handed the two envelopes to his clerk, Velma Smith, who read the verdicts aloud
to the court. The strangulation death of Dominique Dunne
was voluntary manslaughter, and the earlier choking attack a
misdemeanor assault. There was a gasp of disbelief in the
courtroom. The maximum sentence for the two charges is six
and a half years, and with good time and work time, the
convict is paroled automatically when he has served half his
sentence, without having to go through a parole hearing.
Since the time spent in jail between the arrest and the sentencing counted as time served, Sweeney would be free in two
and a half years.

"I am ecstatic!" cried Adelson. He embraced Sweeney,
who laid his head on Adelson's shoulder. Shapiro clutched
Mrs. Sweeney's hand in a victorious salute, but Mrs. Sweeney, of the lot of them, had the grace not to exult publicly
that her son had got away with murder. Then Adelson and
Shapiro clasped hands, acting as if they had freed an innocent
man from the gallows. Not content with his victory, Adelson
wanted more. "Probation!" he cried. As we sat there like
whipped dogs and watched the spectacle of justice at work, I
felt a madness growing within me.

Judge Katz excused the jury, telling them that even though

other people might agree or disagree with the verdict, they must not doubt their decision. "You were there. You saw the evidence. You heard the witnesses." He knew, of course, that they would be hearing from the press about Lillian Pierce in minutes.

He told them that justice had been served and thanked them on behalf of the attorneys and both families. I could not believe I had heard Judge Katz thank the jury on behalf of my family for reducing the murder of my daughter to manslaughter. Rage heated my blood. I felt loathing for him. The weeks of sitting impassively through the travesty that we had witnessed finally took their toll. "Not for our family, Judge Katz!" I shouted. Friends behind me put warning hands of caution on my shoulders, but reason had deserted me.

Katz looked at me, aghast, as if he were above criticism in his own courtroom.

"You will have your chance to speak at the time of the sentencing, Mr. Dunne," he said.

"It's too late then," I answered.

"I will have to ask the bailiff to remove you from the courtroom," he said.

"No," I answered. "I'm leaving the courtroom. It's all over here."

I took Lenny's wheelchair and pushed it up the aisle. The room was silent. At the double doors that opened onto the corridor, I turned back. My eyes locked with Judge Katz's, and I raised my hand and pointed at him. "You have withheld important evidence from this jury about this man's history of violence against women."

The jury foreman, when asked later by the press what finally broke the deadlock, replied on television. "A few jurors were just hot and tired and wanted to give up."

The trial was over. Sentencing was set for November 10.

There was an uproar in the media over the verdict, and KABC radio ran an on-the-hour editorial blasting it. Letters

of outrage filled the newspapers as stories of John Sweeney's
history of violence against women became public knowledge.
The *Herald-Examiner* published a front-page article about the
case: "Heat of Passion: Legitimate Defense or a Legal Loop-
hole?" Judge Katz was severely criticized. In the weeks that
followed, a local television station released the results of a
poll of prosecutors and criminal defense lawyers in which he
tied for fourth-worst judge in Los Angeles County.

Several days after the verdict I returned to the courthouse to
retrieve from the district attorney the photographs and letters
and videotapes of television shows that Lenny had lent him.
The receptionist said I would find Steven Barshop in one of
the courtrooms. As I passed Courtroom D, out of habit I
looked in the window. At that instant Judge Katz happened
to look up. I moved on and entered Courtroom C, where
Barshop was busy with another lawyer. The doors of the
courtroom opened behind me, and Judge Katz's bailiff, Paul
Turner, who had wrestled Sweeney to the ground several
months earlier, asked me to go out into the hall with him.
"What are you doing here?" he asked me. He was stern and
tough.
    "What do you mean, what am I doing here?" I replied.
    "Just what I said to you."
    "I don't have the right to be here?"
    "There's been a lot of bad blood in this trial," he said. I
realized that he thought, or the judge thought, that I had
come there to seek revenge. Then Steven Barshop came out
into the corridor, and the bailiff turned and left us.

In the month between the verdict and the sentencing, we
tried to pick up the pieces of our lives, but the aftermath of
the trial continued. Joseph Shapiro appeared at the wrap party
given by 20th Century-Fox for the film *Johnny Dangerously,*
in which Griffin costars, and the producers asked him to leave
the lot.

According to Proposition 8, the victim's bill of rights, the next of kin of murder victims have the right to take the stand at the sentencing and plead with the judge for the maximum sentence. We were told that Adelson intended to cross-examine us if we did this. We were also told that Adelson, in order to get Sweeney released on probation that day, intended to put on the stand psychiatrists and psychologists who would testify that Sweeney was nonviolent. And we were told that Adelson intended to show a videotape of Sweeney under hypnosis saying he could not remember the murder.

On the day of the sentencing, pickets protesting the verdict, the judge, and Ma Maison marched and sang on the courthouse steps in Santa Monica. Courtroom D was filled to capacity. Extra bailiffs stood in the aisles and among the standees at the rear of the room. A young man called Gavin DeBecker sat next to the bailiff's desk and made frequent trips back to the judge's chambers. DeBecker provides bodyguard service for political figures and public personalities.

Throughout the several hours of the proceedings John Sweeney remained hunched over, his face covered by his hands, so unobtrusive a figure that he seemed almost not to be there.

Two of Sweeney's sisters took the stand and asked for mercy for their brother. Mrs. Sweeney described her life as a battered and beaten wife. Griffin took the stand and presented Judge Katz with a petition that had been circulated by Dominique's friends; it contained a thousand signatures of people protesting the verdict and asking for the maximum sentence. Lenny spoke, and I spoke.

We were not cross-examined by Adelson. No psychiatrists or psychologists took the stand. No videotape of Sweeney saying he could not remember the murder was shown. But a whole new dynamic entered Courtroom D that day and dominated everything else: the outrage of Judge Burton S. Katz over the injustice of the verdict arrived at by the jury.

He mocked the argument that Sweeney had acted in the heat of passion. "I will state on the record that I believe this is a murder. I believe that Sweeney is a murderer and not a manslaughterer. . . . This is a killing with malice. This man held on to this young, vulnerable, beautiful, warm human being that had everything to live for, with his hands. He had to have known that as she was flailing to get oxygen, that the process of death was displacing the process of life."

Judge Katz then addressed Sweeney: "You knew of your capacity for uncontrolled violence. You knew you hurt Dominique badly with your own hands and that you nearly choked her into unconsciousness on September 26. You were in a rage because your fragile ego could not accept the final rejection."

He said he was appalled by the jurors' decision over Sweeney's first attack: "The jury came back—I don't understand it for the life of me—with simple assault, thus taking away the sentencing parameters that I might have on a felony assault."

He called the punishment for the crime "anemic and pathetically inadequate." Having got the verdict we felt he had guided the jurors into giving, he was now blasting them for giving it.

He went on and on. It was as if he had suddenly become a different human being. However, all his eloquence changed nothing. The verdict remained the same: manslaughter. The sentence remained the same: six and a half years, automatically out in two and a half.

Surrounded by four bailiffs, Sweeney rose, looking at no one, and walked out of the courtroom for the last time. He was sent to the minimum-security facility at Chino.

Gavin DeBecker pursued us down the hall. He said Judge Katz would like to see us in his chambers. Lenny declined, but I was curious, as was Griffin. DeBecker led us to Katz's chambers. "Burt," he said, tapping on the door, "the Dunnes are here."

Judge Katz was utterly charming. He called us by our first

names. He talked at length about the injustice of the verdict and his own shock over it, as if all this was something in which he had played no part. He said his daughters had not spoken to him since the verdict came in.

He gave each of us his Superior Court card and wrote on it his unlisted telephone number at home and his private number in chambers so that we could call him direct. What, I thought to myself, would I ever have to call him about?

Back in the crowded corridor again, I was talking with friends as Michael Adelson made his exit. He caught my eye, and I sensed what he was going to do. In the manner of John McEnroe leaping over the net in a moment of largesse to exchange pleasantries with the vanquished, this defender of my daughter's killer made his way across the corridor to speak to me. I waited until he was very near, and as he was about to extend his hand I turned away from him.

When Michael Adelson was asked in an NBC television interview if he thought Sweeney would pose a threat to society when released from prison in two and a half years, he pondered and replied, "I think he will be safe if he gets the therapy he needs. His rage needs to be worked upon." Judge Katz, when asked the same question by the same interviewer, answered, "I wouldn't be comfortable with him in society." Steven Barshop told a newspaper reporter, "He'll be out in time to cook someone a nice dinner and kill someone else." Paul Spiegel, the jury foreman, in a television interview, called the judge's criticism of the verdict a cheap shot. He said the judge was concerned over the criticism he himself had received since the trial and was trying to place the blame elsewhere. Spiegel said he felt that justice had not been served. He said the jury would certainly have found Sweeney guilty if they had heard all the evidence. "If it were up to me," he said, "Sweeney would have spent the rest of his life in jail."

Not one of us regrets having gone through the trial, or wishes that we had accepted the plea bargain, even though

Sweeney would then have had to serve seven and a half years rather than two and a half. We chose to go to trial, and we did, and we saw into one another's souls in the process. We loved her, and we knew that she loved us back. Knowing that we did everything we could has been for us the beginning of the release from pain. We thought of revenge, the boys and I, but it was just a thought, no more than that, momentarily comforting. We believe in God and in ultimate justice, and the time came to let go of our obsession with the murder and proceed with life.

Alex decided to stay with his mother in California and finish his college education. Griffin had to return to New York to start a new film. Lenny became an active spokeswoman for Parents of Murdered Children. I returned to the novel I was writing, which I had put aside at the beginning of the trial.

It was my last day in Los Angeles. I had said my farewells to all, knowing I had experienced new dimensions of friendship and family love. I was waiting for the car to drive me to the airport. Outside it was raining for the first time in months. Through the windows I could see the gardeners of the house where I had been staying in Bel Air. They were watering the lawn as usual, wearing yellow slickers in the insistent down-pour.

There was plenty of time. I told the driver to take me to Crescent Drive first. I wanted to say good-bye to Lenny again. I knew what an effort it had been for her to put herself through the ordeal of the trial. She was in bed watching "Good Morning America." I sat in her wheelchair next to her bed and held her hand. "I'm proud of you, Len," I said to her. "I'm proud of you too," she said to me, but she kept looking at David Hartman on television.

On the way out I took a yellow rose from the hall table.

"I want to make one more stop," I said to the driver.

We went out Wilshire Boulevard to Westwood. Past the Avco theater complex, the driver made a left turn into the Westwood Cemetery.

"I'll be just a few minutes," I said.

Dominique is buried near two of her mother's close friends, the actresses Norma Crane and Natalie Wood. On her marker, under her name and dates, it says, "Loved by All." I knelt down and put the yellow rose on her grave.

"Good-bye, my darling daughter."

The Woman
Who Knew Too Little

SHE WAS A KEPT woman on the skids, an actress-model who neither acted nor modeled, living on the wrong side of town in an apartment from which she was about to be evicted for nonpayment of rent. Amid the half-packed bags and unwanted plants, remnants of a past life bespoke more affluent times: a luxurious, white sofa, a Chinese porcelain dish on a teakwood stand.

He was a homosexual-schizophrenic-alcoholic on the fringes of show business, a collector of celebrities' telephone numbers, who basked for a while in the light of the scarlet woman's illicit fame. They were old friends who had met as patients in a mental hospital and who tolerated each other's transgressions and failures. After he moved in, he found he was buying the groceries and even making the monthly payments on a car she had totaled when she was drunk. She treated him like her slave boy, sending him out to get her bagels and cream cheese, to walk her dog, to find her a new place to live. She spent most of her time in bed, too paralyzed with fear at what was happening to her to function. Her money and glamour gone, she felt that her options for ever recovering her former status had been exhausted. In the end she drove him to the breaking point, and he did for her what she could not do for herself: he killed her.

He waited until she went to sleep. He took her son's baseball bat, adjusted the lights, turned on the water so that the neighbors wouldn't hear anything through the paper-thin walls, and bludgeoned her with the bat until she was dead. She was lying under $500 gray-bordered Pratesi sheets embroidered with her initials, V.M. Next to her bed, on a Formica table, were an empty bottle of Soave wine and a paperback by Carlos Castaneda.

He drove to the North Hollywood police station and confessed. "She wanted to die," he said, and then he gave her credentials, as if seeking approval for the quality of the life he had just extinguished. "Don't you know who she is? Are you aware of her background? It was on the front page of every newspaper because Alfred Bloomingdale was on Ronald Reagan's kitchen cabinet . . ."

Everybody knew the story. Vicki Morgan established herself in tabloid history as the $18,000-a-month mistress of Alfred Bloomingdale, the department-store heir and founder of the Diners Club, when she filed a $5-million palimony suit against the dying millionaire, claiming he had reneged on a promise to provide her with lifetime support and a home of her own. The suit, which sent shock waves through the social world, was instigated after Bloomingdale's wife, Betsy, cut off the corporate checks Vicki had long been receiving. Mrs. Bloomingdale, a leader in Los Angeles and international society and a close friend of Mrs. Ronald Reagan's, refused to be intimidated by her husband's mistress and held her ground throughout the scandal.

The names came pouring out of the killer, a reverential litany of fame and power. People who had never heard of Marvin Pancoast, for that was his name, were part of his confession to the murder of Vicki Morgan.

Pancoast, who didn't usually command much attention, had the detective riveted. In jail two days later, he told a reporter from the *Los Angeles Herald-Examiner* that he expected to be sentenced to the gas chamber. But that was before anyone had heard of the sex tapes. And before he had a lawyer.

Vicki Morgan's fourteen-year-old son attended her funeral at Forest Lawn Mortuary with his Mohawk-cut hair dyed green. The service was sparsely attended, but even as it was taking place, new headlines were in the making. A Beverly Hills attorney announced to the press that he had in his possession three videotape cassettes showing high-ranking members of the Reagan administration in sexual frolics with Vicki and other women.

From Beverly Hills to Washington, in the months that followed, rumors flourished. Wasn't it just too convenient that this woman should end up dead? Broke and at the breaking point, did Vicki Morgan threaten to sell the sex tapes if she was not bought off? Surely, people speculated, Marvin Pancoast had been planted in her house three weeks before her death. Was Pancoast taking the rap for a crime he did not commit—for which he would be found insane, serve a short sentence, and be well remunerated? His clothes had not been blood-spattered after the murder. There were no fingerprints. And the drawers had been ransacked. Where were the tapes? Where was the tell-all memoir Vicki was supposed to be writing?

The murder trial of Marvin Pancoast got under way in June, eleven months after Vicki Morgan's death. When I arrived in Los Angeles, it had already been in the courtroom for three weeks, two weeks of jury selection and a week of prosecution testimony. But it appeared that there was a virtual news blackout on the story.

Although Pancoast had recanted his confession and his lawyers said they would prove that someone else killed Vicki Morgan because she was planning to use the sex tapes for purposes of blackmail, the story was rarely more prominently featured than page 5 or 6 of the *Los Angeles Herald-Examiner*, with hardly a mention in the *L.A. Times* or newspapers around the country. Even the courtroom, in the city of Van Nuys, out in the San Fernando Valley, was never more than half-filled, often considerably less, and most of those people were court watchers. Was this because pressure had been brought to bear to downplay a story that might prove embarrassing to the Reagan administration? Or was it because the stars of the piece were dead and the leading players at the trial had been no more than bit players in the drama, hangers-on and acolytes of the discredited mistress of a disgraced multimillionaire?

Rumor dies hard, though. Shortly after I arrived in Los Angeles, a friend of mine, a movie star, said to me, "Oh, no, darling, Marvin's not guilty. We knew Marvin. He worked for my ex-husband. Nutty as a fruitcake, yes. A murderer, no. You check his mother's bank account after this whole thing is over, and you'll see she's been taken care of for life. They'll just put Marvin in the nuthouse for a few years. It's Marilyn all over again. Did you ever know that the C.I.A. went into Marilyn's house afterward and cleaned out everything? I bet they did that at Vicki's too. That's where the tapes went."

Even at his own trial Marvin Pancoast was not a dominant figure. He has an easily forgettable face, a West Hollywood moustache, and the kind of white skin that turns sunstroke scarlet after five minutes' exposure to the sun. He was always meticulously groomed. Every time he entered the courtroom, he waved to people he knew—his mother, his lawyer's wife, a friend with a ponytail, pierced ear, and turquoise rings on most of his fingers. At times he read *The Shining*, by Stephen King.

Pancoast met Vicki Morgan in 1979, when they were both patients at the Thalians Community Mental Health Center, in Los Angeles. Vicki was there, at Alfred Bloomingdale's expense, for depression following the collapse of her third marriage. Marvin, who had been in and out of such institutions for years, was also in for depression. At various times Marvin had been diagnosed as schizophrenic, manic-depressive, psychotic, and masochistic. They became friends.

He worked in subservient positions for such luminary Hollywood institutions as Rogers & Cowan, the publicists, where he was a gofer, and William Morris, the talent agency, where he operated the Xerox machine. He bragged of knowing famous people in the film business, and his telephone book contained numbers of many celebrated individuals he had never met.

For thirteen months he worked in the office of Hollywood and Broadway producer Allan Carr. "I remember him," said Carr. "He stole my Rolodex with all my celebrity phone numbers, and we couldn't get it back. Finally he sent us back the Rolodex frame, but all the cards were gone."

I remarked to Virginia Peninger, a court watcher seated next to me, that Marvin seemed heavily sedated.

"Oh, he is," she replied. "Ask his mother. She'll tell you. He gets agitated if he doesn't get his medication."

Pancoast had two lawyers defending him, Arthur Barens and Charles "Ted" Mathews, who had been hired by Pancoast's mother and his grandmother. Barens was the star of the courtroom. Trim, handsome, and fashionably dressed, with gold jewelry glistening at each wrist, he drives a Jaguar with initialed license plates and lives on one of the best streets in Beverly Hills. His business card reads: "Arthur Barens, Attorney at Law, A Professional Corporation." This was his third murder trial. Before, he had been mainly a personal-injury lawyer, known as a P.I. He had also worked for years in real estate with Pancoast's mother. A curious twist in his background is that Vicki Morgan, at Pancoast's suggestion, went to ask him to handle her palimony suit after she fired the well-known lawyer Marvin Mitchelson. He admits to having met with her three times, but says that he turned her down because he felt that "she could not possibly win the suit."

Ted Mathews is heavy bellied and wears suspenders. He made no secret of his revulsion for his client's life-style and sexual practices, but he kept pressing home the point that those things should not be brought into consideration when the jury was deciding the guilt or innocence of Marvin Pancoast. Barens and Mathews made an odd couple. In the corridor outside the courtroom, day after day, they titillated a handful of press and television reporters with promises that people who had viewed the sex tapes would appear, that presidential counselor Ed Meese had been subpoenaed, and that Marvin Pancoast would take the stand.

"This whole case is full of people who want nothing more than to have their faces on the six o'clock news," said a disgusted witness as she made her way past the nightly side-show.

"Have you ever represented Marvin before when he has been in trouble?" I asked Arthur Barens.

"Just fag stuff. Lewd-conduct charges," he said.

Representing the prosecution was Deputy District Attorney Stanley Weisberg. Wry, wise, probably witty in circumstances other than these, he was without flash, glamour, or fancy rhetoric. He stuck to the facts. While Barens and Mathews could talk about a police cover-up, the sex tapes, blackmail, hypnosis, drugs, and unnamed higher-ups in the administration, Weisberg had nothing more to go on than Marvin Pancoast's confession. As the days went by, Weisberg became the favorite of the court watchers.

Presiding over the court was forty-two-year-old Judge David Horowitz. Fair and unbiased, he never allowed his courtroom to turn into a circus. When evidence of the existence of the sex tapes was not forthcoming, he disallowed the defense claim that Vicki Morgan was using the tapes for purposes of blackmail, and sustained all objections of the prosecution when the defense asked hearsay questions about the tapes.

One of the most fascinating aspects of the case was the colossal ineptitude of the police work. No fingerprints were taken at the scene of the crime. An officer lamely explained that since Marvin Pancoast had confessed, the police didn't see any point in taking prints. Nor did they seal the house afterward; therefore, anyone possessing a key had access to it in the days following the murder—a strange state of affairs in a case in which missing tapes, both audio and video, played such a large part. The coroner testified that when he arrived at the murder scene at seven o'clock in the morning, he was not able to examine the murder weapon, the baseball bat, for blood, skin, or hair, because the police had sealed it in a plastic bag. It is an almost elementary fact of police work that evidence containing blood, or any body fluid, is never wrapped in plastic, only paper or cloth, because plastic creates a humidity chamber in which bacteria grow and destroy such evidence as blood and tissue. "If this is not an inept police investigation, then it's a deliberate cover-up," said Ted Mathews.

Far more revealing and potentially dangerous than any of Vicki's lurid testimony in the deposition for her palimony suit, in which she recounted in detail the sadomasochistic sexual practices of Alfred Bloomingdale, were her accounts of the personal conversations she had had with Bloomingdale. "Alfred continuously confided in me by telling me his private opinions about influential and important people with whom he was intimately involved, such as Ronald and Nancy Reagan, and he would relate specific instances involving them; and he told me about his involvement in secret and delicate matters such as campaign contributions for Mr. Reagan."

In the second week of the trial, Pancoast's lawyers called a writer named Gordon Basichis to the stand. Basichis had been working with Vicki Morgan on *Alfred's Mistress*, her revenge memoir about her affair with Bloomingdale. Basichis had been introduced to her by a film producer for whom Basichis was writing a screenplay, and with whom Vicki Morgan had had an affair during her affair with Alfred Bloomingdale. Basichis is married to a television executive, has an eighteen-month-old son, and had been working with Vicki for eight months preceding her death. He is dark and intense, and on the stand was sweaty and nervous.

The contract drawn up by Morgan's lawyer, Michael Dave, provided that Basichis was to deliver to her the first chapter of the book plus an outline of the remaining chapters by August 1, 1983. If she disapproved of the material, she had no obligation to proceed with Basichis or compensate him.

Almost immediately after meeting, Basichis and Morgan began a love affair. Eight months after the contract between them was signed, despite nearly daily contact, the initial chapter and outline were still not written. There is some argument as to how many hours of microcassette audiotape were recorded. Vicki's mother, Connie Laney, and Marvin Pancoast, who moved in with Vicki three weeks before her death, recalled that there were many hours of recorded conversations. The tapes were kept in a safe-deposit box to which both Vicki and Basichis had keys. After Vicki's death, when the tapes were ordered to be turned over to the estate, only six hours of tape were forthcoming. What happened to the other tapes, if there were others, has never come to light. Basichis says the six hours of tape he submitted were all that were recorded. What exactly he and Vicki did during the eight months of their collaboration remains a mystery.

One week before her death Vicki Morgan broke off her romantic relationship with Basichis and fired him as her collaborator. A fight occurred, and there were two versions of it. Basichis admitted to having pushed Morgan around. Vicki's mother said Vicki told her that Basichis had hit her and punched her in the face. There were black-and-blue marks on her face and body. In Marvin Pancoast's confession, he said about Basichis, whom he referred to as the writer, "He beat the shit out of her."

The police did not question Basichis until three months after the murder—and then only after being prompted by a reporter—even though he was Vicki's known lover, her known collaborator, and thereby privy to the secrets of her life; even though it was a documented fact that she had fired him and that he had fought with her and struck her.

Basichis denied on the stand that he was responsible for the black-and-blue marks on Morgan's face and body. He denied feeding her Valium habit or buying her cocaine. He said that he and Vicki had made up on the night before her death and that he had spent the night with her. He said that on the following night, the night of the murder, he was home with his wife watching the All-Star Game on television, which his wife later corroborated on the stand.

"How often did you go to bed with her?" Barens asked him.
"I didn't keep count."

When a break was called, Basichis stood up and walked across the courtroom to where I was sitting. "Hello," he said, and called me by my first name. I was stunned. Later he told me he had submitted a manuscript of one of his early books to me in 1976, when I was a film producer.

"They're trying to pin this murder on me," Basichis said, talking rapidly into my ear. He kept jabbing his finger into his shirt collar. "I didn't kill her. I swear to you. I was deeply in love with her. I would never harm her."

"Who do you think killed her?" I asked him.

"Marvin," he answered, and then added, "with help."

"Help from whom?"

He shrugged and did not reply. His dislike of Arthur Barens and Ted Mathews was matched only by their dislike of him. Barens and Mathews said on television and to the press that Basichis was a definite suspect, a drug taker, and a drug supplier to Vicki, and that he might possibly have made a deal with "someone" to turn over the missing audiotapes based on his eight months of conversations with Vicki. Basichis said that Barens's relationship with Vicki Morgan had involved more than just three office meetings.

That night Basichis called me at my hotel and asked if he could see me. He said he had things to tell me and offered to let me read *Alfred's Mistress*. I asked if we could talk on the telephone, and he said that his telephone might be tapped. He arrived more than an hour late, after his wife had called to say that he had lost his credit cards and money but that he would be there.

Basichis rarely completes a sentence. He begins, thinks of something else, switches to it. He talked nonstop for two hours. His nervous presence was compelling, a frightened man masquerading under a tough bluff, but when the tape of our meeting was transcribed, by a woman in Santa Monica who was so shocked by the profanity she left blank spaces, page after page read like incoherent ramblings. He claimed there were no videotapes of Vicki Morgan cavorting with government officials. He said he would have known if there had been, because he and Vicki had spent so much time together. He said, "She had a sense of vanity that went so deep she wasn't going to spread herself out among a whole bunch of those guys in their white fleur-de-lis boxer shorts."

When he left my hotel room after midnight, I read *Alfred's Mistress*. It had, he told me, been turned down by his publisher because another writer, one of seven doing a book on the same subject, had told the publisher that Basichis was the murderer.

Basichis hadn't completed even the first chapter of *Alfred's Mistress* during the eight months of his collaboration with Vicki Morgan. He wrote the book sometime after her death in July 1983 and before Marvin Pancoast's trial for her murder in June 1984. When he showed it to me in June, it had already been rejected by ten publishers.

It is a curious book, told completely in the third person, as if the eight months of conversation, taping, and lovemaking between the author and the deceased has not taken place. Some of it is culled from the deposition that Vicki filed at the time of her palimony suit. Her meeting with Bloomingdale, their first assignation, his sadomasochistic tendencies, and the financial terms of their long affair were all things I had read about before. Some of the other facts in the book are inaccurate: a depiction of Mrs. Bloomingdale as foulmouthed is totally off the mark. Most important, none of the big administration names that had long been whispered as having connections with Vicki are mentioned; there is nothing in the book that would embarrass the administration.

It is Vicki Morgan's life story. It tells of her three marriages (her first ex-husband went to jail for dealing drugs in order to make enough money to win her back from Bloomingdale). It tells of her love affairs with the convicted financier Bernie Cornfeld, the King of Morocco, and a Saudi Arabian princess, as well as of a romance with Cary Grant.

Most compelling is the picture of Bloomingdale, caught in

the grip of living a double life, too involved with each to let go of the other. A scene where Bloomingdale tells Vicki that he had cancer as he is leaving for England with his wife to attend the festivities connected with the royal wedding of Prince Charles and Lady Diana, and a scene where Bloomingdale is carried to Vicki's house by a male nurse for their final lunch, for which Vicki spent $1,000 on flowers and appointments for what she called her "Betsy table," made crystal clear the complicated nature of their relationship.

"What about all this stuff she was supposed to have known concerning campaign contribution and personal things about people in the administration?" I asked Basichis.

He said her information was fragmented—pieces of a story, but not the whole story. Most of what she knew, he said, was more embarrassing than dangerous, gossip about the private and family lives of top figures.

The book tells her history, but it doesn't explain her. What did she have, this girl? What was her allure? Why did a king fly her to Rabat? Why did a princess charter a yacht to sail her to Honolulu? Why did a man who had everything risk it all on her? I once saw her at the Christmas party of a film-company business manager. "That's Alfred Bloomingdale's girlfriend," the daughter of one of Alfred Bloomingdale's friends told me. What I remember most about her were her eyes, taking in everything from the sidelines, meeting the looks of people who looked at her. Friendly-aloof. And pretty. But Hollywood parties are full of pretty girls who are somebody's girlfriend.

The moot point of the trial remained the celebrated sex tapes. There was not a person in the courtroom who had not heard that a certain member of the administration was supposed to be shown on them dallying with Vicki, with pink carnations in his pubic hair. But where were they? Do they exist? Did they ever exist? The main source of information about them was Marvin Pancoast, known to be pornography-mad. Could they have been a figment of his imagination? Vicki's close friend of fourteen years, Sally Talbert, said under oath that she had never heard Vicki mention the tapes. Even Gordon Basichis, everyone's enemy in this story, said Vicki never mentioned the tapes to him. The first public mention of the tapes was by Robert Steinberg, who was, for twenty-four hours, Marvin Pancoast's lawyer. Two days later, when asked for proof that the videotapes existed, Steinberg said that he had seen them, but that they had been stolen from his office. Later Steinberg was indicted for filing a false robbery report. When the defense called him to the stand during the Pancoast trial, he took the Fifth Amendment nine times because the misdemeanor charges for the robbery report were still pending.

A secretary from William Morris who knew Pancoast when he worked there said she had heard about the tapes a year and a half before Vicki died. This woman, who wished to remain anonymous, believes they did exist. She also believes that Pancoast definitely struck the fatal blows. "Marvin's craving in life was to be famous. The people Marvin had been in contact with all the time in the business have what Marvin has an absolute blood-lust for: they are famous. It goes beyond rich. I believe he's guilty. I have from the outset. Marvin's motive for killing Vicki was convoluted but to his mind very logical. She represented one of his closest links to the spotlight because of Bloomingdale. This made her a star to Marvin. When she no longer had the backing that made her a star, she began to lose value to him. That was reason enough for him to kill her, that she wasn't famous anymore.

"The last time I visited Marvin in jail," she said, "he had on his lap a file folder of all the newspaper front pages that he had been on, and he was stroking that folder and showing me, 'Look, I'm on the front pages.' If that folder had been a human being, it would have had the most incredible orgasm of its life. I thought to myself, I have now seen obscenity. I didn't go back to see him again. I couldn't."

On July 5, after only four and a half hours of deliberation, the ten-woman, two-man jury returned a verdict of guilty of murder in the first degree. They believed the confession on the night of the murder, and the defense had not proved that the all-important tapes ever existed or that a conspiracy had taken place. The defense's contention that Gordon Basichis had held Vicki Morgan's Doberman pinscher while an unknown assailant delivered the fatal blows and then had hypnotized Pancoast into thinking that he had killed Vicki—this drew muted guffaws in the courtroom—apparently held no weight with the jury either.

Arthur Barens reported that Marvin Pancoast was devastated by the verdict. As he was led from the courtroom by bailiffs, Pancoast, who had sat through the trial in medicated silence, snapped at a photographer taking his picture, "Fuck off, man. Leave me alone."

From his cell in Los Angeles County Jail, Pancoast told a psychiatrist that he believes that Betsy Bloomingdale and Ronald Reagan are in a conspiracy against him and that he is being monitored by the F.B.I. and the C.I.A. through radios and television sets.

The same day that Pancoast was convicted, a full-page, color picture of Betsy Bloomingdale cutting roses in the garden of her Holmby Hills Palladian villa appeared on the cover of W. The article, about her widowhood, was called "Betsy in Bloom." Van Nuys, where the trial took place, on the other side of town, was farther away from her than New York or London or Paris. She is the survivor of this story.

Vicki Morgan was the victim twice over. She was only thirty when she died, and only seventeen when, according to her, the fifty-four-year-old Bloomingdale picked her up in a Los Angeles restaurant by pressing an $8,000 check into her hand. Their liaison lasted twelve years, starting the day Vicki joined Bloomingdale and several other women for a bout of sadomasochistic play and ending with his death, when she said of his wife, who had interred him privately without any announcement to the press. "She buried him like a dog."

Vicki Morgan was a mistress who led a mistress's life. She shopped and spent while a limousine waited with a driver to carry her packages. She worked on her tan, took social drugs, took acting lessons, and went to the same hairdresser that the wives of Bloomingdale's friends went to. She drove expensive cars, but she never had a pink slip of ownership. She lived in expensive houses in fashionable areas, but she never had the deed to a house. She heard secrets that could have made her solvent for life, but, sadly for her, she couldn't remember most of what she heard.

Candy's Dynasty

IT IS NO SECRET that the movie rich live rich. What is less well known is that the television rich live even richer, because, except for a few film people like Ray Stark, Steven Spielberg, and George Lucas, the television rich *are* richer than the movie rich. And more flamboyant. While the movie rich have settled into the relatively conservative habits of "old money," the television rich, long considered second class in the rigid caste system of filmland society, are bringing back to Hollywood a way of life and a standard of living that have not been around since what are nostalgically referred to as "the great days," when big spender William Randolph Hearst built Marion Davies a castle in the sand at Santa Monica.

The name on every lip and in every column these days is Candy Spelling, wife of television supermogul Aaron Spelling, who is reputed to be the most successful, most powerful, and richest independent producer in Hollywood. In a community inured to tales of extravagant life-styles, Candy Spelling is setting new perimeters. Recently the Spellings paid $10,250,000—in cash—for the cream-colored stone mansion Bing Crosby owned when he was married to Dixie Lee. Then, after discussing plans for structural changes with some of the priciest architects on the West Coast, they decided to tear the 43,000-square-foot house down to the ground and start again from scratch. "What she ended up with is a $10,250,000 lot," commented one of the outraged neighbors. The new house will be even bigger and will include, when it is completed in two years, an indoor ice-skating rink, a bowling alley, and a zoo. Before a curtain is hung or a carpet is laid, Aaron Spelling will have spent close to $25 million on it.

Stories about Candy Spelling have reached mythic proportions. They say she wears $4-million worth of jewels to lunch, and that she carries her own jeweler's loupe when she attends auctions at Sotheby's. They say that one Christmas Eve a couple of years ago, studio teamsters drove all night with truckloads of snow in order to cover the lawns of her estate so that the Spelling children could have a white Christmas. That when she walks on the beach at her Malibu house, she has been known to send a nanny ahead to plant rare and beautiful shells in the sand so that her daughter can find them. That when she and her husband are in Las Vegas, where they vacation, in the Presidential Suite of the Desert Inn surrounded by bodyguards, they have slot machines brought up to their rooms. That she once summoned dress designer Carolina Herrera to fly her latest collection and three models from New York to Las Vegas for a private fashion show and then bought the entire collection, including bags and hats. That her five-year-old son wears a monogrammed smoking jacket. That the Lucite invitations to her New Year's Eve party were so heavy they each cost $1.47 in postage to mail locally. And on and on.

The source of this bounty, fifty-nine-year-old Aaron Spelling, grew up in poverty in a Texas ghetto, the son of a Russian immigrant tailor. He wore hand-me-down clothes, and was called Jewbaby by the local bullies. I first knew him in the mid-fifties, when we worked together on "Playhouse 90"; Aaron was a sometime actor and fledgling writer, I was the assistant to the producer. Shy and socially insecure, he seemed a highly unlikely candidate for success, power, and multimillionairedom. In the early sixties, we connected again at a film studio called Four Star, where he was already on his way as a television producer, creating such series as "Zane Grey Theater" and "Burke's Law."

In the 1983–1984 season Aaron Spelling's shows represented a record seven hours of network-television prime time,
all on ABC. His company, Aaron Spelling Productions, of
which Candy Spelling is secretary and treasurer, produced
"Dynasty," "The Love Boat," "Hotel," and "Matt Houston,"
and under the Spelling-Goldberg banner he produced "Hart
to Hart," "Fantasy Island," and "T. J. Hooker." The man has
turned out thousands and thousands of hours of film, including more than ninety motion pictures for television. Every
hour of every day his series are playing in syndication somewhere. Estimates of Aaron Spelling's income by industry ob-
servers exceed $20 million annually.

Candy married Aaron Spelling nearly sixteen years ago.
Before that she had worked briefly as a hand model, by some
reporters as a salesgirl at Saks, and as an interior decorator.
Both of them had been married before. His first marriage, to
actress Carolyn Jones, lasted eleven years. Candy was very
young at the time of her first marriage, about which little is
known.

My several encounters with Candy over the years have
been brief but vivid. On one occasion I was producing a
television film about Hollywood climbers for her husband's
company, and we were shooting on location in a Sunset Boulevard mansion a few blocks from the Spellings' house. It was
late, and we had just one sequence left to shoot, an exterior
scene showing extras arriving at a Hollywood party dressed in
evening clothes and furs, when we discovered that by mistake
the wardrobe had been returned to the studio. I made an
emergency call to Candy's house and told her the jam we
were in, and she sent her driver over with enough fur coats
from her fur vault to dress all the extras.

During that same period I ran into her at a Hollywood party
and admired an armload of diamond bracelets she was wearing. "This one's for 'The Rookies,' " she said, ticking them
off playfully, "and this one's for 'The Mod Squad,' and this
one's for 'Starsky and Hutch.' "

Another time she called to ask me about a beach house that belonged to a film-star friend of mine. She had heard it was going to be up for sale, and she wanted to get inside and have a look.

"The thing about that house," I said, "is it's not very beachy. It's more like a Beverly Hills house at the beach."

"That's perfect!" said Candy without any hesitation, and I remember thinking to myself at the time, These people are getting rich.

After not being in touch with them for years, I wondered if Candy would see me for an interview. I was informed that it was a very busy period for her. She was preparing for her first trip to Europe, which required extensive planning. Because her husband will not fly, they were going to travel to the East Coast in a private railroad car with a chef, a maid, a nanny for each child, guards, and her majordomo. For the ocean crossing, they had reserved a cluster of suites on the *QE2*. She was also involved in the spring fair at her children's school, and she was organizing a benefit dinner for her favorite charity, the fight against retinitis pigmentosa. Moreover, she runs several businesses in addition to being an officer of her husband's company. But she agreed to be interviewed.

The Spellings live in Holmby Hills, a small enclave of superaffluence north and south of Sunset Boulevard between Beverly Hills and Bel Air which contains some of the most extravagant dwellings in the United States. Their house, like most houses in the area, is protected from the prying eyes of tourists and curiosity seekers by a wall, gates, and electronic surveillance. Across the street from the entrance, an old lady sitting under a black umbrella sells guide maps to the movie stars' houses. Within walking distance are the homes of Burt Reynolds, Barbra Streisand, Gregory Peck, and Rod Stewart.

Outside the gates on a steel pole set into the asphalt is an intercom over which I announced my name and business to a guard inside. A closed-circuit television camera was trained on me; then the wrought-iron gates swung open. The driveway goes uphill to a courtyard. At the top of the hill was a black-and-white Los Angeles police car, which I later learned is a permanent fixture, pulled from one of Spelling's television series to discourage the uninvited. Spelling has given his neighbor, producer Ray Stark, a similar one for his courtyard. Beyond were two white Lincoln limousines, one for Aaron, one for Candy. An armed guard waved me up to the entrance of the mansion. He accompanied me to the front door and unlocked it, and I entered the lavish world of Candy Spelling.

It is a world of big houses, big cars, big jewels, big parties, and Big Plans. It is not merely rich, it is "Dynasty"-rich, and I felt I was stepping into a television set and becoming a character in an episode of that series. Either Blake and Krystle Carrington are based on Aaron and Candy Spelling, or Aaron and Candy Spelling are based on Blake and Krystle Carrington.

Candy's publicist received me, and Candy's secretary, seated behind an antique desk in the library, made polite conversation. The majordomo—the chief steward of a noble house, according to the Random House dictionary—passed busily through the room. The butler stood at attention by the door, appearing not to listen, waiting, one supposed, for orders. (In the course of the afternoon he periodically brought us fresh Tabs in fresh Baccarat glasses to replace Tabs in Baccarat glasses that we had barely touched.) We were all minor players in the episode, setting the scene for the arrival of the star.

"Hello," Candy said, ten minutes later, walking into the room, holding out her hand, moving like a woman who is coming from an important engagement and will soon be leaving to go to another. She is not the sort of rich woman who languishes in luxurious indolence. There are lists in her head of things to be done; a household to oversee, businesses to be run, menus to be planned for the chef of the chartered railroad car, blueprints of the new house to be checked, an art class to be taught at her children's school, a cocktail party at Chasen's for her husband's company.

She is thirty-seven years old, slender, sleek, manicured, exercised, massaged, well dressed, and very glamorous. She was nervous about being interviewed. She said she had been savaged by a national magazine last year and had cried for a week afterward. She laughed when I reminded her of our past encounters. Her speaking voice has the regionless sound of those models who have speaking lines in cosmetics commercials. It is probably a voice in transition. Her conversation is full of film references. For example, she says "lap dissolve" to denote the passage of time in a story she is telling: "Aaron promised his mother that as long as she was living he would never fly in another plane. Lap dissolve. She's no longer living, but he's now built it up in his mind he's going to die the next flight he takes."

Chain-smoking cigarette after cigarette, she told me her back story. She grew up in Beverly Hills affluence. "We lived right next door to Barbara Stanwyck," she said. "There were four in help in the house, and I was allowed to cross the street to play with my girlfriend only in the company of a maid."

As she spoke, she changed, almost imperceptibly, the position of a vase holding a spray of cymbidium blossoms. Telephones and doorbells rang, and she went right on talking as if she had heard nothing, knowing that messages would be taken. When Candy was eight, her father, who was in the furniture business, suffered severe financial reversals, and the family moved to an apartment in the area known as South of Wilshire. She took buses to school for the first time and learned to cook. She looks upon those years as the most important in her life, for they taught her, as she puts it, "what the dollar meant, where it had to go, and what you had to do with it." She began to read the *Wall Street Journal* as a child.

She has a computerlike mind for the factors and figures concerning anything that interests her: television, orchids, architecture, furniture, travel. She can tell you the advan-

tages of having the screen in her new projection room rise
from the floor rather than lower from the ceiling. She can
describe to you the difficulty of installing a Dolby sound system. She can explain precisely why she has had the floor plans
and elevations of her new house made up at the scale of a half
inch to a foot. She knows that the private railroad cars fueled
with propane cannot travel farther east than Chicago, and
she knows which cross-country train routes offer the best
sightseeing with the fewest number of stops.

On her finger was one of the greatest jewels in the world, a
pear-shaped, D-flawless, forty-carat diamond, purchased from
the estate of the late Shah of Iran. She can explain, with the
expertise of a gemologist, the color gradations of diamonds
from D, the highest, through I.

"How do you know all this?" I asked.

"I can just look at a diamond and tell you exactly how
many carats it has," she answered.

"But how?"

"I've been told I have a better eye than the late Harry
Winston," she said.

She talks constantly about her husband and children. "We
don't like to go out a lot, to social parties. We love our house,
and we love being home together with our family, and it
makes a lot of sense to have everything we love the most
around us."

On the piano is a silver-framed color photograph of the two
Spelling children, five-year-old Randy and eleven-year-old
Tori, an aspiring actress, who has guest-starred in twelve ep-
isodes of her father's television series. In the photograph, the
children are standing on the winding stairway in the front
hall, wearing eighteenth-century, French court costumes with
powdered wigs, jewels, and shoes with buckles.

"What was the occasion?" I asked.

"Halloween," she replied, adjusting the position of the
frame by a fraction. "Nolan designed those costumes."

Nolan is Nolan Miller, her personal couturier and the designer of the clothes worn by Joan Collins and Linda Evans

Dominique Dunne

Dunne family portrait, Christmas 1964. Dominick and Lenny Dunne with, from left, Griffin, Dominique, and Alex.

District Attorney Steven Barshop points to bruises inflicted on Dominique Dunne by John Sweeney five weeks before the assault.

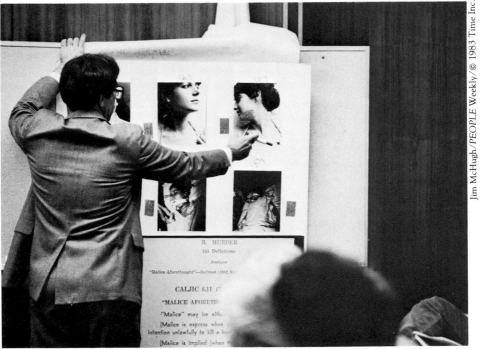

John Sweeney at his trial for the murder of Dominique Dunne. He was convicted of manslaughter. In the foreground is his defense attorney, Michael Adelson.

Judge Burton S. Katz presided over the trial of John Sweeney. The jury found his instructions to be incomprehensible.

Vicki Morgan, mistress of Alfred Bloomingdale, murder victim of Marvin Pancoast, and the woman who knew too little.

"Peace is a transcendent state," says Mrs. Marcos, in exile in Hawaii. "I was a soldier for beauty and love. I was completely selfless. They say about me that I was extravagant, but I gave."

Imelda serves Ferdinand home cooking in Honolulu, still wearing her $300,000 engagement ring.

Candy and Aaron Spelling, the Krystle and Blake Carrington of Beverly Hills. "I can just look at a diamond," Mrs. Spelling says, "and tell you how many carats it is."

Without the Beverly Hills Hotel, Muriel Slatkin was like King Zog without Albania.

Ivan Boesky's father-in-law considered him a bum and a ne'er-do-well, but in an intrafamily coup he ended up controlling the Beverly Hills Hotel.

Swifty Lazar has not gotten to the top of the heap in Hollywood and remained there for almost four decades by being a softie.

on "Dynasty," as well as the clothes on five other Aaron
Spelling series. Candy owns 50 percent of his business, Nolan
Miller, Ltd. She also owns, with her partner, Marcia Lehr, a
successful boutique in Beverly Hills specializing in party planning, antiques, and gifts, in which she is an active participant
and buyer. Gifts for guest stars on all of Aaron's shows come
from her boutique. Party favors at her own parties are so
plentiful she provides bags that match the tablecloths to carry
them home in.

"What exactly is your input in 'Dynasty'?"

"The books," she replied.

"The books?"

"I go over the books."

She knows if money is being wasted, and where. She understands costs and schedules and overtime and double time.
Aaron comes home late in the day to spend time with the
children. Often she returns to the studio with him at night to
watch the dailies and rough cuts of his movies and series.
Aaron is said to rely greatly on her opinions, both financial
and creative. She has an eye for discovering talented young
people. An insomniac, she does most of her work after midnight, when the house is quiet.

She claims to relax by straightening out, in meticulous
color sequence, "from white to cream to bone to beige, from
lemon to yellow, from pink to red," the blouses and slacks in
her mirrored and marbled dressing room. She does the same
in her husband's closets, where the socks are strictly separated, the brown in one drawer, the blue in another, the black
in a third.

"Will all this furniture go in your new house?" I asked.

"Oh, no. Just the antiques."

"Who will be your decorator?"

"I will," she said.

The new house, country French in style, will make Blake
and Krystle Carrington's place on "Dynasty" look like a guest
house. It will be 360 feet long, or, as the majordomo explained, "longer than a football field." The house is fulfilling

a lifetime dream, which includes the double staircase she has
wished for since she first saw *Gone With the Wind*. She knows
exactly what she wants; she has already arranged most of the
furniture on outsize floor plans, and she is in the process of
picking fabrics and colors and papers even though construction is just getting under way. "I'm going to need a thirty-
eight-inch table here and an eight-foot sofa there," she said,
pointing at the plans. She has sent her architect to France to
study, not the great châteaux in the country, but the large
new houses "in whatever the Bel Air or Beverly Hills of
France is."

Even the Spellings' philanthropy has elements of a scripted
television drama, with a beginning, a middle, and an end.
Watching the news with Aaron one night last year, Candy
was moved to tears by the story of a black college student
named Derrick Gordon, who was suffering from a hereditary
heart disease that had already killed an older brother. He
needed a heart transplant, and his family still needed to raise
$100,000 more for the operation. The Spellings had their
accountant issue a check for the entire amount, and their
driver delivered it along with $500 worth of steaks to the
Gordon family. When Aaron received an N.A.A.C.P. Hu-
manitarian Award three months later, Derrick Gordon was
among the honored guests on the dais.

Except for Saturday nights, when the Spellings show films to
a small group of intimate friends, Candy's entertaining is almost exclusively business-oriented. She claims she has no
social ambition, although the dining table in her new house
has been designed to seat twenty-eight. Their appearances in
public are mostly at wrap parties celebrating the completion
of a film or series, testimonial dinners, charity benefits, industry galas, and the Golden Globe, Emmy, and Oscar awards.
For these occasions Candy is ablaze with jewels from her
famous collection. She has sets in all the colors.
    Following in the tradition of the great film moguls of an

earlier time, the Spellings have started a racing stable of thoroughbreds and are regulars at the track. Recently Candy's attention has also turned to art. The pictures in her present house are not top-drawer and will probably not make the move to the new house. Her husband's partner, Douglas Cramer, a noted collector of contemporary American art, tried to influence her in the direction of his taste, but she is said to have been much more taken with the Impressionist collection of Mrs. William Goetz, the daughter of the legendary Louis B. Mayer and for forty years the leading *grande dame* and hostess of the film industry. "I said to Aaron," reported Candy, "let's cool it on the jewels for a while and get into art." A few days later they bought a Monet, their first major picture.

Imelda in Exile

DIRECTLY UNDER my balcony at the Kahala Hilton hotel, porpoises frolicked in a pool. Beyond them, past the palm trees blowing in the breeze, a Secret Service man was patrolling the beach with a bomb-sniffing dog. Out in the calm Pacific, flanked by two more Secret Service men in bathing attire, Secretary of State George Shultz was enjoying a 6:30 A.M. swim. Two other Secret Service men, in blue blazers and beige slacks, carried walkie-talkies and stared back at the balconies of the hotel.

After a few moments the secretary of state came out of the water, dried himself with a towel, and walked back to the hotel, encircled by his attendants, one of whom let his surveillance of the balconies flag long enough to observe the playful activities of the porpoises in the pool. In Honolulu on a two-night stopover, Mr. Shultz was on his way back to Washington from the summit meeting in Tokyo, via Manila, where he had called on the new president of the Philippines, Corazon Aquino. The previous day a reporter had asked him if he intended, while he was in Honolulu, to call on the former president of the Philippines, Ferdinand Marcos, and his wife, Imelda, who were in temporary residence less than two miles down the beach from the Kahala Hilton. "No!" the secretary of state had snapped.

Later Mr. Shultz went further and publicly rebuked Ferdinand Marcos for using his safe haven in Hawaii as a base from which to foment difficulties for President Aquino's government. "He is causing trouble," said Shultz, and Jaime Cardinal Sin, the archbishop of Manila, echoed the secretary of state's remarks. The cardinal said that Marcos was financing demonstrations against Mrs. Aquino, and in some cases paying people 100 or 150 pesos ($5 or $7.50) to dress up as priests and nuns in order to attract favorable press attention for him abroad. The Marcoses were definitely in Dutch.

For four days I had sat on my balcony over the porpoises, waiting for Imelda Marcos to respond to my request for an interview. Contact with the former first lady of the Philippines had been made for me, not through political or diplomatic connections, but through friends of hers in high society. For as everyone now knows, in addition to being the first lady for twenty-one years and the chatelaine of Malacañang Palace, Imelda Marcos had been a card-carrying member of the jet set, numbering among her friends Lord and Lady Glenconner, the British aristocrats, who are friends of the royal family; the Count and Countess of Romanones, members of the Spanish nobility; Princess Firyal of Jordan; the Agnelli and Niarchos families; and American multimillionaires like David Rockefeller and Malcolm Forbes. In recent years, however, those closest to her had been less socially exalted: Adnan Khashoggi, the Arabian billionaire, for whom she entertained extravagantly in her New York mansion; Cristina Ford, the Italian-born former wife of Henry Ford; George Hamilton, the suave and debonair Hollywood actor, and his mother, Anne; Van Cliburn, the acclaimed pianist; and Franco Rossellini, of the New York and Rome film world.

On my arrival in Honolulu, I had written her a personal note. For four days it had gone unheeded. I had seen Mrs. Marcos once during that time, but from a distance. The previous Sunday, Mother's Day, also happened to be the thirty-second wedding anniversary of the Marcoses, and a real estate broker in Honolulu who had been instrumental in finding a house for them to live in told me that the local pro-Marcos Filipino-American community was planning a celebration in their honor. I arrived at the Blaisdell auditorium at eleven A.M. to ensure getting a seat and stayed until the program ended, at five in the afternoon.

Of the 115,000 Filipinos in Hawaii, approximately 15,000
are pro-Marcos, and most of those are from Ferdinand Marcos's home province of Ilocos Norte. The crowd of cheering
Filipinos in the auditorium that day was estimated at between
four and five thousand, and the event was long and tedious.
Children from the Hawaii Talent Searchers Club sang Cyndi
Lauper and Huey Lewis vocals to instrumental tracks recorded
on cassettes. There was a demonstration of ballroom dancing
by a gray-haired woman and a younger female partner. Following that was a magic act, and then, to the delight of the
audience, a leading pop star called Anthony Castillo, who
had arrived from Manila the day before to take part in the
festivities, sang a medley of songs.

When Ferdinand and Imelda Marcos arrived, about an hour
before the end of the celebration, the crowd waved V-for-
victory signs to them and broke into song:

> *We love you, Mr. President,*
> *First Lady, and family.*
> *We thank God for you again,*
> *For what you are and what you'll be.*
> *Our country is more beautiful*
> *Because of you and what you did.*
> *We who are here will be with you.*

Despite all the cheering, the Marcoses appeared subdued.
Mrs. Marcos, dressed in the same green dress, black patent-
leather shoes, and matching pearl costume jewelry that she
had worn for every public appearance since her arrival in
Hawaii, blew desultory kisses at the crowd. Then she took
the microphone like a nightclub artiste and began to sing.
She knew how to work the stage, playing first to one side,
then to the other, and even though her famous singing voice
was woefully out of tune, she did not seem to care. Her eyes

had a distant look. Next the president came forward and joined her in a Philippine love song. Taller than her husband, Mrs. Marcos easily upstaged him. There seemed to be no intimacy between them; they were together only in the sense of being side by side.

Before the speeches became political and the anniversary celebration turned into what sounded like the opening of a campaign to return Marcos to power, a speaker rose and told a long and rambling anecdote about longevity in marriage. He said that once when Henry Ford was asked to what he attributed the success of his long and happy marriage, he replied, "I have never changed models." The speaker added triumphantly that Mr. Marcos had never changed models either. The speaker was, it turned out, talking about the grandfather of the present, thrice married Henry Ford. One of international society's favorite and most persistent rumors over the years has been about Mrs. Marcos's supposed romantic attachment to a member of the Ford clan, on whom she is said to have showered gifts of jewelry, but obviously the rumor was unknown to both the teller of the Ford anecdote and the audience that delighted in his story. In a country where poverty is endemic, the Marcoses' wealth—their real estate holdings, their jewels and paintings, their extravagant entertaining—has always been an extremely sensitive issue. Yet, for the most part, the people cheering for them that day were the poor of the Philippine community in Honolulu. The comparison of Imelda Marcos to Evita Perón is said to distress Mrs. Marcos, because Evita Perón started her rise as a prostitute, but the fact remains that Imelda Marcos inspires a similar adoration in some of her subjects.

When Mrs. Marcos moved to the microphone to speak, her listlessness evaporated. She spoke in her native language, sprinkled with occasional English words, like *security guards* and *television crews.* After a few moments she was crying, and many in the audience were crying too. She extended her arms above her head and, with tears streaming down her face, said in English, "When I hurt, I do not cry, but I cry when you overwhelm me, and you have overwhelmed me." As theater, it was a magnificent moment.

Then Mr. Marcos made a speech in the dialect of his province, Ilocos Norte. "As your elected president," he began, and when that brought cheers he reiterated: "*As your elected president . . .*" But he had already been completely overshadowed by his wife.

On my fifth morning in Honolulu I received a call from Mrs. George Ariyoshi, the beautiful Japanese-American wife of the governor of Hawaii. Old friends of the Marcoses', the Ariyoshis had placed friendship before political considerations in going to Hickam Air Force Base in February to greet and place leis around the necks of Imelda and Ferdinand Marcos when they arrived from Guam after being forced to flee the Philippines. The gesture brought criticism down on Mr. Ariyoshi, and if he had not been a lame-duck governor it might have proved disastrous; the people of Hawaii did not want the Marcoses to settle there and did not let up in their demands for them to leave. Although the two couples ceased to see each other publicly, Mrs. Marcos and Mrs. Ariyoshi remained friends and talked every day on the telephone. I had been invited to lunch with Mrs. Ariyoshi the day after I arrived, and I was hoping that she had been able to appeal to Mrs. Marcos on my behalf.

Mrs. Ariyoshi informed me instead that Mrs. Marcos would not see me. She assured me it had nothing to do with me personally; it was just that a policy had been made against interviews. She said that Mrs. Marcos was sorry I had made the trip from New York for nothing. If I called the Marcos house immediately, she said, Mrs. Marcos herself would explain why it was impossible. Mrs. Ariyoshi had done all that she could do.

When I called, Mrs. Marcos came immediately to the telephone. She was strong-voiced and definite. She had not, she reminded me correctly, ever promised me an interview. "The problem," she said, "is that it is premature for me to give interviews at this point in time. With all these cases pending against us all over the world, an interview might prejudice people against me. This is not the right time for me to give my side of the story. There is such an overwhelming force against us. As much as possible we would like to keep our silence for the time being."

"I'm sorry, First Lady," I replied. (I had been told to address her as either First Lady or Ma'am by someone better acquainted with protocol than I.)

"Our life is so disorganized," she added, and the finality in her voice sounded a bit less final.

"At least I can say when I go back that I saw you, First Lady," I said.

"But I don't go out. Where did you see me?" she asked.

"I went to the celebration of your thirty-second wedding anniversary at the Blaisdell auditorium on Sunday."

"You did?"

"Yes."

"Why?"

"I wanted to see you and the president."

"When were you there?"

"I was there for all five hours."

"But we didn't come until the end."

"I had no way of knowing that."

She hesitated for a moment, then asked, "Where are you staying?"

"At the Kahala Hilton."

"It's down the beach from where we are."

"I know."

She hesitated again. "I will meet you," she said. "What time is it?"

"It's twenty minutes past nine."

"At ten o'clock. There must be no pictures."

"Fine."

"No tape recorder."

"Fine."

"No questions. This is not an interview."

"Fine."

"And only," she concluded, "for ten minutes."

She gave me the address: 5577 Kalanianaole Highway. Of course, I already knew where she lived; everyone in Honolulu knew. I had driven by the house every day since I had been there, and once I had parked my car nearby and walked along the beach to the Marcoses' place. I was able to look through the shrubbery and stare at the house for fully five minutes before two guards, sitting on chairs and chatting together, noticed me. The security provided by the state had been taken away from the Marcoses three and a half weeks after they arrived in Hawaii; these guards were part of a volunteer security force made up of pro-Marcos members of the Filipino colony in Honolulu. They had walkie-talkies but no guns that I could see; however, when I realized that they had spotted me, I quickly turned and walked away.

A Hawaiian real estate agent claimed to me that the Marcoses owned two homes in the fashionable Makiki Heights section of Honolulu, one worth $1.5 million and the other worth $2 million. The houses are said to be in the names of two well-to-do Filipinos. The Marcoses cannot admit owning the houses, for fear the present Philippine government will put a claim on them. Because of the Marcoses' political unpopularity, it had been hard to find anybody anywhere who would rent to them. For example, an approach had been made through an emissary for the Marcoses to rent one of the great houses on the fashionable Caribbean island of Mustique, but because Mustique is a favorite vacation retreat for members of the British royal family, it was thought that the Marcos presence might prove embarrassing. However, according to a prominent resident of the island, if the United States were to request that they be given haven, or if the Marcoses were to make a proper gesture, such as building a $65 million airstrip on nearby Saint Vincent, new consideration for their future welfare in Mustique might be taken into account.

•   •   •

They pay $8,000 a month for the house they finally did find, and since they have a severe cash-flow problem, brokers are on the lookout for a house at half that rent in case the Marcoses are forced to remain in Honolulu. Each Sunday after mass, which is said privately for them in the house, members of the pro-Marcos Filipino community in Honolulu arrive with food, flowers, and money for the couple and their entourage.

In the beginning of their stay, demonstrators collected in front of the house with signs saying, MARCOS, MURDERER, GO HOME or HONK IF YOU WANT THE MARCOSES TO LEAVE. To the distress of the neighbors, the honking went on all day and all night. Since the bombing attack on Libya and the nuclear fallout at Chernobyl, however, the press has turned its attention away from them, and the demonstrations have stopped, but the former first family remain in a sense incarcerated, behind locked gates.

In a sane real estate market, the Marcos house would be described as an $80,000 or $90,000 single-family dwelling on valuable beachfront property. There are neighbors close by on both sides, with no walls or fences between the houses. Shrubbery and a high wooden fence with two gates that are kept locked at all times protect the house from the highway. I waved and yelled through the fence, and the gate was finally opened when I made it clear that Mrs. Marcos was expecting me. Five or six old cars littered the short driveway. Parking was difficult, and the guards were unhelpful. The entrance to the single-story, shingle-roofed, ranch-style house was visually marred by an electric blue tarpaulin strung up haphazardly between two trees to protect the guards from the sun. Beneath it stood a wooden table and a couple of chairs. On the table were a plate of ripening mangoes and several empty Pepsi-Cola cans. One had a sense of "there goes the neighborhood" about the place.

Entering the small front hallway, a visitor is immediately confronted with the presidential seal, which fills an entire wall. Next to it on a pole is the flag of the Philippines. The house consists of a living room, a dining room, a kitchen, three bedrooms, a maid's room, three bathrooms, and a lanai, a sort of porch furnished like a living room which is a feature of most Hawaiian houses. Next to the house is a separate one-room guest house. There are, I learned, more than forty people living here. Most of the original furniture has been removed and replaced by rented furniture. A plain, wooden table on the terrace was covered with a white plastic table-cloth and surrounded by card-table chairs with MGN RENTAL stenciled on the back. In the living room were several television sets, a VCR, and both audio and video recording equipment. (A Honolulu rumor has it that the Marcoses ruined their friendship with President and Mrs. Reagan by videotaping a private conversation they had with them and later giving the tape to television stations.) An upright piano and a synthesizer were pushed against the wall of the lanai. On practically every table surface, there were mis-matched bouquets of tropical flowers, many wrapped in aluminum foil or tied with homemade bows, unwatered, dying or dead. There were flies everywhere. All the books on the tables, with the single exception of David Stockman's *The Triumph of Politics*, were by Ferdinand Marcos, including *The Ideology of the Philippines*.

About a dozen men in Hawaiian shirts were seated about the room. In a gray suit, shirt, and tie, I felt overcitified. President Marcos, we were told, had a toothache and was at the dentist, but the first lady would be with us presently. For the first time it occurred to me that all the people there had been summoned, as I had, to see her. I made conversation with a Filipino journalist from New York who had worked in the consulate when Marcos was in power, and with Anthony Castillo, the pop singer from Manila, who told me that one of the first things Corazon Aquino had done was abolish all the cultural programs started by Imelda Marcos. All the artists in the country, he said, stood behind the Marcoses.

And then the first lady entered the room, the strong scent

of heady perfume preceding her. She moves in an extraordinarily graceful manner; even in those simple rooms she was like a queen in a palace. All of those seated jumped to their feet the moment her presence was felt. As if a party line of "stay poor and lie low" were in force to counteract the stories of excess that had dominated the media for months, Mrs. Marcos was again dressed as she had been dressed on every public appearance since she arrived in Hawaii: the green dress, black patent-leather shoes, and pearl earrings and ring which were obviously costume jewelry. Her black hair was majestically coiffed.

She gave instructions to a servant to offer coffee to everyone. She greeted a university professor and discussed briefly a paper he was preparing. She exchanged affectionate words with a group of Filipinos who had come from California and New York to participate in the wedding-anniversary celebration. People addressed her as either First Lady or Ma'am. She pointed out to another visitor a huge color photograph in an ornate gilt frame of the president and her with their children and grandchildren which had been an anniversary gift. I understood before she came to greet me that I was part of a morning levee, one of a group being offered an audience and a few words of greeting. She offered her hand. Her crimson fingernails had been carefully manicured with white moons and white tips. She is, at fifty-seven, still a beautiful woman. We exchanged a few unmemorable words. When I conveyed greetings from the people who had brought me into contact with her, she indicated that I should take a seat on the lanai. Then, on instructions from her that I was not aware of, the room cleared and we were alone.

Imelda Marcos had been described to me by a friend who knew her well as a woman who understood luxury better than anyone in the world. Flies buzzed around us in great profusion, but she seemed not to notice them. She never waved them away. I had the feeling that she had simply ceased to pay any attention to the surroundings in which she was living. There is a sense of tremendous sadness about her, but if she is at times despondent, she manages to shake herself into positive pursuits. Was this the same woman who had boogied the nights away in the various private discotheques of her various private residences with her jet-set friends, wearing a king's ransom in jewels on her wrists, fingers, neck, and bosom?

Stories of Imelda Marcos's extravagance abound. "Please, for God's sake, don't use my name," several of her former friends said to me. People in society are notoriously loath to have their names quoted in stories about events in which they have participated, although they don't mind filling you in on the details. Former houseguests at Malacañang Palace tell how the streets of Manila were cleared of people when Imelda took them about the city, and how the guest bathrooms in the palace were so well equipped down to the smallest luxury items that ladies even found packages of false eyelashes in their medicine cabinets. They tell how Imelda abolished mechanized street cleaning in Manila and dressed the homeless of the city in yellow-and-red uniforms and provided them with brooms and the title Metro Aide—instead of street cleaner—so that the streets would be immaculate around the clock.

On a balmy evening a little over a year ago, Malcolm Forbes gave a dinner cruise around Manhattan aboard his yacht, the *Highlander*, in honor of Mrs. Marcos. While the party was still in progress, a lady-in-waiting went around the ship and issued impromptu invitations to a select number of Mr. Forbes's guests to continue the party back at the first lady's New York town house on East Sixty-sixth Street. On arriving there, guests were taken up to the sixth-floor discotheque, where an enormous supper had been laid. The amount of food on display was said to be embarrassing—ten entrées to choose from, including lobster and steak. Since they had all just eaten Malcolm Forbes's sumptuous buffet, they had to pass up Mrs. Marcos's food, choosing instead to dance to the live orchestra that awaited them. As the festivities came to an end and guests started leaving, Mrs. Marcos proved again that there were inner circles within inner circles by asking a few people to stay behind so that she could show them the private floor of her mansion, where her bedroom and sitting room were. Two large, leather caskets, each about the size of half a desk, were brought out by maids. Each contained seven or eight drawers filled with jewelry, which were emptied onto the floor so that the remaining guests could try them on. That was said to be her favorite late-night entertainment, to forestall going to bed. A Madison Avenue jeweler who specializes in estate jewelry told me that Mrs. Marcos had a passion for canary diamonds until last year, when the color yellow became associated with the ascendancy of Corazon Aquino. The town house was furnished out of a Park Avenue triplex maisonette that had belonged to the late philanthropists Mr. and Mrs. Leslie R. Samuels. Mrs. Marcos had tried to buy the triplex for $9 million, but she was turned down by the co-op board of that building because her presence would have posed too great a security risk. Instead she bought the entire contents of the enormous apartment so that she could do up the Sixty-sixth Street town house in just a few days in order to be ready for a party she was giving for Adnan Khashoggi.

Although she was reverential about royalty, she had been known to upstage the crowned heads she revered. She once arrived at a party for the shy and retiring Queen of Thailand, for example, with her own television crew to film her being received by the queen. On another occasion, at a small private party at Claridge's in London attended by the former King Constantine of Greece, Mrs. Marcos arrived to the cheers of London's Filipino community, who mysteriously materialized outside the hotel right on cue.

"The last two and a half months," Mrs. Marcos said, looking around the plain rooms filled with rented furniture, "have been so enriching. This is a good period for enlightenment. I have no bitterness in my heart."

Disinclined to be questioned, she was more than inclined to talk, and for the three and a half hours that the promised

ten minutes eventually stretched into, she talked nonstop on
a variety of topics, as if she had been starved for conversation.
If I sometimes asked things that she did not wish to comment
on, she kept talking as if she had not heard me. Thirty minutes into our visit, I asked if she minded if I wrote down
something she had said so that I would be able to record her
words accurately. She didn't respond yes or no, but she didn't
ask me to stop writing either, and from that moment on her
whole manner and delivery changed. I felt I was watching a
well-rehearsed performance as she expounded at great length
on the subject of love, couched in a series of mystical,
Rajneesh-sounding philosophical phrases.

"Beauty is love made real," she said. "Beauty, love, and
God are happiness and peace. Love has only one opposite.
The opposite of love is not hate. The opposite of love is
selfishness. A human being has three levels: his body, his
mind, and his spirit. In the spiritual world, you find peace,
and none of this matters." She gestured expansively with her
hands and arms to indicate her surroundings. "I am completely devoid of basic human rights, but I am blessed. Everything we have here comes from the people. All our valuables
were impounded. We do not have a single dollar. What can
you pick up in an hour's time when you are told to pack up
and leave? Your whole lifetime is exposed to the world.

"Peace is a transcendent state. I was a soldier for beauty
and love. I was completely selfless. They say about me that I
was extravagant, but I gave. Your magazines and papers say
that I bought art. It is true. I bought art, but I bought art to
fill our museums so that people could enjoy beauty.

"I was born in a family that gave much of themselves in
love. There were eleven children. I married a president. I was
the first lady for twenty-one years. Very few have been as
privileged as I have. If you are successful and have everything,
destiny has a way of imposing money, power, and privilege
on you.

"Across the sea is my country, and sometimes when I sit

here, I think that I can see it. This house is very modest, but your real home is the home within. I am so glad that I have one good dress and one good pair of shoes. Now I don't have all that hassle about clothes and what to wear."

Long stretches of this material I had seen her deliver on tapes left behind in the Sixty-sixth Street house in New York. The irony was that on the tapes she had been expounding her philosophy in a champagne toast to the munitions entrepreneur Adnan Khashoggi.

Her face is unlined and looked to me unlifted. "People say I have spent a fortune on plastic surgery," she said, understanding my stare, "but I have not. The only time I thought of having it done was to cover this scar from the assassination attempt on my life." She held up her arm and showed me the ugly scar from a knife wound inflicted on her in 1972. "My husband said to me at the time, 'Don't have it covered. Wear it as your badge of courage.' Once Queen Elizabeth said to me, 'Imelda, how did you live through it?' "

Mrs. Marcos looked past me but continued talking. I assumed that I had lost her attention and that it was time to leave. She was, in fact, looking at her daughter Irene, who had come out onto the lanai and indicated by gesture that there was a telephone call for her. "This is my beautiful daughter," she said, her face filled with love as she looked at her. They exchanged a few words in Pilipino. "I'm so sorry," she said. "I must take this call. It's Margot Fonteyn." Dame Margot Fonteyn had helped Mrs. Marcos found the ballet company of Manila. For that, Mrs. Marcos had given her an award with a pension attached to it. She gave a similar award and pension to Van Cliburn.

Several times she evinced a mildly gallows-type humor. Speaking of the *tsunami,* a tidal wave from the Aleutian Islands that had threatened to devastate Honolulu a few days earlier, she told how a helicopter had hovered over the house while a man inside shouted orders on a bullhorn to them: "Pack your clothes and get out!" "But we just did that in

Manila," she said she had told her family, and she laughed as she recalled the story.

Trapped in a Catch-22 situation, the Marcoses were broke. Their tangible assets, including the money and jewelry they entered Hawaii with, had been frozen by the U.S. government. Talking about the generous Filipinos in Honolulu who bring them food and clothing, she said, "They even bring me shoes." In the manner of an expert storyteller, she let a few seconds pass and then added, "Who knows, soon I may have three thousand pairs."

Again Mrs. Marcos looked beyond me to someone entering. "Oh, here comes the president," she said. Out onto the lanai walked Ferdinand Marcos, surrounded by aides. He no longer looked the way he had during his last days in office or when he got off the plane at Hickam Air Force Base outside Honolulu, as if he were going to die later in the day. His color was healthy; his step was sure. He was wearing a three-piece suit of beige gabardine with a white shirt, cuff links, and tie, but he was still a far cry from the dynamic world leader who had held total control over 50 million people for twenty-one years. Mrs. Marcos rose and walked toward him. When she introduced me to him I sensed he was displeased to find a journalist in his house with notebook in hand. Later, thinking back, it occurred to me that if I had stayed for only the ten minutes that the visit was supposed to be, I would have been long gone before the president returned from the dentist.

"How is your tooth, Ferdinand?" asked the first lady, like any wife concerned with her husband's welfare and, at the same time, distracting him.

"You know, Imelda," he replied, speaking English in a high-pitched, singsong fashion and pointing to a tooth in his open mouth, "it wasn't my tooth after all. There was a fish bone in my tooth. The dentist took out the fish bone, but he didn't take out the tooth." The president was delighted with his story, and all his aides laughed appreciatively. Mrs. Marcos joined in. They actually seemed for a moment like a

Filipino Ma and Pa Kettle. Then the president excused himself, saying he had to return to work with his lawyers.

After he left, she spoke proudly of him. Sometimes she
called him Marcos, sometimes "the president," sometimes just
"my husband." "My husband wrote two or three dozen
books," she said, "including *The Ideology of the Philippines*—
the only world leader to write an ideology of his country.
Your media," she said, in the scoffing tone she used every
time she mentioned the U.S. press and television coverage of
their downfall, "said that Marcos's medals from World War II
were fake. But his medals were awarded to him by General
Douglas MacArthur. Is General Douglas MacArthur a fake
too? Your media says that my husband had no money when
he became the president, that he became rich in office by
stealing from the Treasury. That is completely untrue. My
husband was a flourishing lawyer in Manila for years before he
became the president." She walked out of the lanai into the
living room, disappeared down a short hallway, and returned
almost immediately. "Let me show you the only thing I kept,"
she said, placing a large diamond ring in my hand. "This is
my engagement ring from thirty-two years ago, eleven years
before he became the president. You can see from this ring
that my husband wasn't exactly poor then." She told me that
the jewelry firm of Harry Winston had appraised the ring
several years ago at $300,000.

After I handed the diamond ring back to her, she again left
the lanai. This time she returned with another thing she had
obviously kept, one of the world's most famous diamonds,
called the Star of the South, which she said the president
have given her for their twenty-fifth wedding anniversary.
She said it was listed in the Harry Winston book, and it is.
The kite-shaped, 14.37-carat, D-color diamond has belonged
to the late Evalyn Walsh McLean, the owner of the ill-fated
Hope diamond, as well as to the Duchess of Windsor's great
friend Mrs. George F. Baker. The Winston book says that the
jeweler sold it again in 1981—two years after the Marcos's
twenty-fifth wedding anniversary.

It had been widely reported that the gangs of international social figures who had danced in her discotheques and been recipients of her bounty had, for business or social reasons, deserted her in her decline and disgrace. A host of one of the major, upcoming, international society balls said, "We were going to invite Imelda, but, you know, it's less easy now." Another onetime friend said, "I'd like to call her, but it's bad for business."

"Have you been disappointed by your friends?" I asked. She looked at me but did not answer. "Have you heard from them?"

She replied slowly, choosing her words. "Those who had our telephone number in Hawaii, yes. Those who had the time, yes. But this is when you find out who are your real friends, and this is when you cut out the fakes." Again she thought for a time and then added, "I have no bitterness in my heart."

"Do you suffer when you read what is said about you in the press?"

"I don't read anymore what they say about me. I only read straight news. I am not a masochist. I am a very positive human being. I have so much energy that I sleep only two hours a night. In the end we will be judged by history, not what they write about us now.

"I want to show you something," she said. She called inside to have a television-and-VCR set rolled out onto the lanai. Anthony Castillo, the pop singer, operated the machine for her. She wanted me to watch a tape that had arrived a few days before from the Philippines, showing pro-Marcos demonstrations in Manila, which, she said, had become daily occurrences in the city even though the Aquino government would not grant permits for such demonstrations. She obviously knew every frame of the hour-long tape and, snapping her fingers, gave frequent, excited instructions to Castillo. It was suddenly easy to see her as a woman used to giving orders and used to having them obeyed.

"Go forward. More. More! Stop here. Listen to what these people are singing: 'You can imprison us, but you cannot imprison our spirits.' That's their song. There are a million people in that crowd. Go forward. More. Go to the demonstration for Mrs. Aquino. Stop! Look at *her* crowds. The people are just not there for her. Mrs. Aquino is an out-and-out Communist. America doesn't want to believe this, but it is true. The minister of labor is a Communist. Go forward. To the nuns and the priests. Look at them. 'Marcos,' they are yelling. Nuns. Look here, Mr. Dunne, do you see that woman? She is a famous film star. All those people there are artists and writers. All the creative people are for Marcos. Go forward. Watch here. See that child on the shoulders of his mother? The Communist Mrs. Aquino's soldiers are going to shoot that child. Watch. Listen to what they're saying about Cardinal Sin. They say, 'Cardinal Sin is the officer in charge of hell!' "

When the tape ended, we sat for a few moments in silence. "Would you like to see my house?" she asked. In the kitchen a half-dozen women were preparing lunch, setting out big plates of mismatched food, like a potluck dinner. "The people here bring us our food," she said, exchanging greetings with the women. "Two people sleep on the floor of this room," she said, opening the door of a tiny laundry room with a washer and dryer. She then opened the door of the maid's room. Lined up on the floor were canvas cots, and there were women asleep on several of them. She walked in and stood in the small space between two of the cots. "Sixteen women sleep in here," she said. "In shifts. The nurses and the women in the kitchen and the others." The sleeping women slept through her talking.

We next walked through the garage. On a shelf were a pile of unopened legal-looking envelopes. "Look," she said, pointing to them and then holding them up for ridicule. "Do you know what these are? They're subpoenas. We're being sued by people all over the world. Even my daughter is being sued.

Even my baby grandchild! Someone thinks valuables and Philippine currency were smuggled out in the baby's clothes." She shook her head at the lunacy of it. I followed her as she walked along a cement walkway between the garage and the one-room guest house next to it. "Forty-two men sleep in this room," she said, indicating it with a toss of her head.

"There were forty-two, Ma'am," said the chief of the guards. "There are only fifteen here now."

Inside were rows of cots with clothes piled on the floor beside each one. Some men were eating, some were sitting on their cots, some were sleeping. It was hot, and the room smelled. It looked like an enlisted men's barracks badly in need of inspection. The men stared out as we stared in.

Mrs. Marcos moved on across the lawn, stopping to look for a moment at a neighbor next door. No greeting passed between them. We went in the side entrance of the house and were in the hallway to the three main bedrooms. One bedroom was his. One was hers. Six people slept in the third bedroom, including the Marcoses' eight-year-old adopted daughter, Aimee, the grandchild of Mrs. Marcos's late brother and sister-in-law. A vibrant personality in the belea-guered household, Aimee had the previous Sunday patiently fanned Ferdinand Marcos in the hot auditorium during the anniversary proceedings. Their daughter Irene and her husband and children have their own house elsewhere. When I asked where her daughter Imee, a former member of Parliament, and her son, Ferdinand junior, the former governor of the province of Ilocos Norte, who is known as Bongbong, were, she did not answer. I had heard rumors that they were in Mexico seeking a haven for the family. The hallway was full of suitcases, piled high one on top of the other, cheap blue plastic cases next to expensive Louis Vuitton cases—the old kind of Louis Vuitton cases, before they were mass-marketed. On one bag was a tag saying "Mink Coat."

"We won the election by a million and a half votes," she said, becoming impassioned again, "but the world media makes Mrs. Aquino look like Joan of Arc." Her loathing of

Corazon Aquino was evident in every word. "Even the people in her own province voted for my husband. She was the underdog because of Karma. She has abolished the constitution. What she is is a dictator. They are beginning to discover just how far to the left she is."

She found a book about herself that she had been searching for. Page after page of it was filled with her cultural and political accomplishments. "I have been in more corridors of power than any woman in history," she said. "I have been received by every head of state, including two Russian heads of state. Only five months ago I was received by Gorbachev. I went to Tripoli and personally made a treaty with Qaddafi, the only treaty that he has ever honored."

She turned the pages of the book. "I had this building built in a hundred days," she said. "Our Cultural Center, which I commissioned, was built before the Kennedy Center and the Sydney Opera House. Reagan, when he was still the governor of California, came over to dedicate the center. I founded the University of Life. President Giscard d'Estaing came himself to see my University of Life so that he could build one in France. Today the literacy rate of the Philippines is 90 percent, and the literacy rate of the city of Manila is 100 percent!" A further litany of her accomplishments followed: "I planted . . . I founded . . . I built . . . I commissioned . . . I opened . . . I had composed . . . I began . . ."

She paused dramatically. "Do you read about any of that in your papers? No. Your magazines showed a picture of me, saying, 'Mrs. Marcos was blazing in diamonds and rubies.' " Her voice was filled with scorn. "What they don't understand was that the necklace was false. They are pop-in beads. I'll show you. I've got them here. Most of the jewelry I wear is imitation, made by the artisans and craftsmen of my country." I looked at her incredulously. Just then a maid passed through the front hall, where we were standing, and Mrs. Marcos spoke to her in Pilipino. When the maid returned, she was carrying six or seven necklaces, each in a stiff plastic case with snaps. "Look at these," said Mrs. Marcos. She handed me the cases of necklaces, and I put them on the seat of a chair and knelt down to look at them. I do not know if they were imitation or not. Certainly they were beautiful, and the workmanship was extraordinary. On one necklace, canary diamonds alternated with pink diamonds. She said that the settings had been dipped in gold so that they would not turn her neck black.

"I thought you weren't able to keep any of your jewelry," I said.

Mrs. Marcos replied that these necklaces were left behind in Malacañang Palace when they fled, and that Mrs. Aquino had no interest in them because they were imitation. Later they were stolen from the palace. A friend of hers in Manila recognized them, bought them for 20,000 pesos, or $1,000, and sent them to her in Honolulu.

At that moment, from behind a small louver window looking out from the hall onto the front porch, came the words, "I'm listening, Imelda," loud and clear. The window opened vertically, and Ferdinand Marcos, displeased, was framed in it. In an instant, Mrs. Marcos whipped off a shawl from her shoulders and threw it over the cases of necklaces, covering them. "My husband doesn't like me to show the jewelry," she whispered to me. There was urgency in her voice. The president came out the door, and I felt ridiculous as I stood up in front of the chair to block his view. In another instant Mrs. Marcos was at his side. She took his hand affectionately. "Do you know, Ferdinand," she said, "Mr. Dunne has written a best-selling novel that is going to be made into a film in Hollywood."

"Oh?" he said, smiling. "In Hollywood!"

In a wonderfully complex moment of stunning social pyrotechnics, Mrs. Marcos had diverted her husband's attention and also acknowledged for the first time that she knew things about me. We chatted pleasantly, and then the president excused himself, saying he had to get back to work on one of the many lawsuits pending against them.

"How much is this one for, Ferdinand?" she asked.

"Oh, twenty-four billion," he joked, and they both laughed.

It was time to leave. We shook hands good-bye. "For four hundred years we were a subject people," she said. "When Marcos became president, we had been independent for only twenty years. We were a mixture of races. We had to identify who we were. We helped our people to understand what it meant to be a Filipino."

Beverly Hills Coup

"It's *KING LEAR,* isn't it?" said the person on the telephone discussing the drama of the Silberstein sisters with me.

"King Lear?" I asked.

"You know. Goneril and Regan, that sort of thing, with the father manipulating it all."

"I see."

In truth, I had not thought until then of Goneril and Regan, but I had thought of another sister act, closer to Beverly Hills, where the Silberstein drama was unfolding: the Mayer sisters, octogenarian Edith Goetz and septuagenarian Irene Selznick, whose father, Louis B. Mayer, the legendary movie mogul, by favoring one in his will and ignoring the other, contributed to their well-known dislike of each other, a dislike refueled recently in Mrs. Selznick's memoir, *A Private View.*

In the case of the Silberstein sisters, Muriel Slatkin and Seema Boesky, their father, Ben L. Silberstein, a Detroit real estate magnate and hotel tycoon, left them equal shares—48 percent each—in the world-famous Beverly Hills Hotel, the current market value of which has been estimated at around $125 million. Alas, he left the remaining 4 percent to his sister in Detroit, and therein lies the story.

In the early 1950s, the tale goes, when the girls were teenagers, their father took them and their mother to the hotel for the first time. The opulent structure, which had been built in 1912 and long referred to affectionately as the Pink Palace, dazzled young Muriel, representing glamour and beauty to her in a way that Detroit never had. She is reputed to have said to her father, "Daddy, if you want me to be interested in your business, why don't you buy this hotel?" And Ben Silberstein, who doted on Muriel, did just that, for the then outrageous price of $5.5 million. He bought it from Hernando Court-right, the colorful owner, a bona fide member of Los Angeles society, whose financial backers included such prominent fig-ures of the film world as Loretta Young and Irene Dunne. The plan was for Courtright, who knew everyone, to stay on for five years as president and general manager.

The relationship between the cigar-chomping Ben Silber-stein, who dressed in knit shirts and slacks, and the elegant Hernando Courtright, who sometimes wore serapes and sombreros, was strained from the start, and their distaste for each other turned to downright hatred when Silberstein, after divorcing his wife, fell in love with Courtright's wife, Rosalind, a nightclub chanteuse, and later married her. Courtright went on to buy the Beverly Wilshire Hotel, which he proceeded to turn into a first-class rival to the Beverly Hills Hotel.

Silberstein's marriage to Rosalind Courtright was short-lived. In anticipation of its collapse, he moved his official residence to Florida in order to avoid California's community-property laws, which would have allotted half of his earn-ings during the period of the marriage to his wife. In Palm Beach, following his divorce from Rosalind, Silberstein met and eventually married a beautiful former show-girl-turned-socialite named Bonnie Edwards, whose numerous husbands have included playboy Tommy Manville, the asbes-tos heir and tabloid darling of the period. The marriage of Ben and Bonnie endured, and they resided most of each year in the Beverly Hills Hotel, where Bonnie Silberstein became much loved by the staff and the community.

Silberstein was always referred to as Mr. S. by the staff so that guests would not realize he was the owner. To the sur-prise of all, he never accepted large groups or conventions, as the other big hotels did, and he was dedicated to preserving the country-club atmosphere that made the Beverly Hills such a famed gathering place for film stars, visiting royalty, and the power elite of Hollywood. But he never lost his abrasive manner.

One morning at breakfast in the coffee shop, General David Sarnoff, president and chairman of the board of RCA, said to Silberstein, "I spend so much time here, you should give me a discount."

"I'm thinking of charging more for people who stay here too long a time," replied Silberstein.

In the meantime, the Silberstein sisters, Muriel and Seema, both married Detroit boys. There had always been a degree of friction between the sisters, possibly even fostered by their father, who was said to favor Muriel, and their marriages brought this friction to the surface. Their father was delighted with Muriel's choice, Burton Slatkin, whose family ran a jewelry store, but not remotely pleased with Seema's choice, Ivan Boesky, whose family owned a couple of Brass Rail restaurants. Burt Slatkin quickly became the son Ben Silberstein never had, and went to work for his father-in-law at the Beverly Hills Hotel. As for Ivan Boesky, anyone who knows the family will tell you—and none more graphically than Muriel—that Ben Silberstein considered him a bum and a ne'er-do-well, destined to amount to nothing. "My father was always disappointed with my sister's choice of husband," Muriel told me when I first contacted her. She is an attractive woman in her early fifties, dark-haired, with a svelte figure, of whom a friend has said, "What's on Muriel's mind is on her tongue." "I was *not* my father's favorite, as people say, but my father approved of my husband and despised Ivan. I was always the peacemaker in the family, and I would say to my father, 'Don't make Seema miserable because you don't approve of her husband.' "

A public indication of the low esteem in which Ivan Boesky was held can be inferred from Sandra Lee Stuart's book *The*

Pink Palace, a gossipy history of the hotel published in 1978,
a year before Ben Silberstein's death. In the book Ivan Boesky
is never mentioned by name, and his wife is dismissed in these
nonprophetic words: "Silberstein's other daughter, Seema,
now Mrs. Seema Boetsky of New York, is not involved in the
hotel." The name Boesky is even misspelled.

In 1973 Burt Slatkin became the president and chief operating officer of the hotel, although he was still answerable to
his father-in-law. The Slatkins had two sons, Tom and Edward, and it was the dynastic wish of Silberstein that these
two grandsons, who received their education in hotel administration, would someday run the place. With the help of
Silberstein, Muriel and Burt built, on Beverly Hills Hotel
property which was deeded over to them, the kind of house
that can best be described as a showplace—a Regency mansion with a copper mansard roof and a courtyard designed by
the eminent Los Angeles architect Caspar Ehmcke, and a
perfectly puffed-pillowed interior designed by the prestigious
William Chidester.

With a fortune, a mansion, and a hotel behind her, Muriel
Slatkin had more credentials than most to make it as a social
figure in Beverly Hills. She was never asked to join the Amazing Blue Ribbon, the ultimate distinction for women of social
achievement in Los Angeles, but she had a double cabana at
the Beverly Hills pool, where she entertained important visi-
tors for lunch, and she always occupied the same table in the
celebrity-filled Polo Lounge. Her parties at home, famous for
the extravagance of the food, were duly reported on in the
society pages of the *Los Angeles Times* and *Herald-Examiner,*
as well as in the gossip columns of the *Hollywood Reporter* and
Daily Variety. She took tables at all the major charity events
and gave cocktail parties for famous writers stopping at the
hotel on their book tours. She even had a brief film career,
playing a San Francisco society matron in Allan Carr's movie
Can't Stop the Music. When she became actively involved in
the redecoration of the hotel, she was given an office near her

husband's, and she had pink-and-green bordered business cards made up proclaiming her proprietor of the Beverly Hills. The hotel became her principality, and every time she walked in or out of it, everyone, from the doorman on, bowed to her and treated her like a princess.

Like her father, she was not universally loved, although her supporters are passionate in her defense. A complaint often heard about her is "She's the type who's your best friend one day and looks right through you the next." However, like her or not, everyone in Beverly Hills took cognizance of Muriel Slatkin.

While Muriel became a personality in Beverly Hills, Seema lived in New York with her husband, whom she adored, and their four children in a large Park Avenue apartment provided by Ben Silberstein. In contrast to Muriel, who sought out recognition, Seema worked hard at remaining anonymous. A trim-figured, high-spirited woman with dark hair and vibrant blue eyes, Seema bears a strong resemblance to her sister. While her relatives in Beverly Hills downplayed her husband's business abilities, others, nearer to the mark by far, described Ivan Boesky as a late bloomer. With the emergence of arbitrage on Wall Street, the man whose in-laws had considered him a bum unquestionably found his vocation. Arbitrageurs are, according to a December 1984 article about Boesky in the *Atlantic*, "professional gamblers who bet on the outcome of corporate transactions. They invest in securities that are the subject of an announced tender offer, a merger, or a liquidation, and then realize a profit in the spread between their purchase price and the selling price when the announced event is consummated."

In 1979 Ben Silberstein became ill, and his illness exacerbated the trouble between the sisters. Muriel went to the U.C.L.A. Medical Center every day to visit her father and complained to anyone who would listen that Seema should have spent more time there too; she felt that Seema was not carrying her share of the load. Silberstein left each daughter 48 percent of the Beverly Hills, and before he died, in an effort to provide a secure future for the hotel he loved, he advised Muriel to give half of her shares to her husband, Burt. Bonnie Silberstein, Ben's widow, who had grown closer to Seema than to Muriel, received an apartment on Sutton Place in New York, an apartment in Palm Beach, and visiting privileges in the Beverly Hills Hotel, but, contrary to popular belief, no shares in it. The remaining 4 percent went to Ben Silberstein's sister, Gertrude Marks, of Detroit, and her two children.

Burt and Muriel Slatkin offered to buy the 4 percent from Gertrude Marks, but they balked at the price she asked. That was a fatal error. "Burt's tight," explained a close observer of the situation to me. "He lost the fucking hotel because he's tight. When you're in a takeover, you don't quibble about money. If the old lady wanted a hundred bucks, you give her three, and if she wanted a million bucks, you give her three million. That's what his brother-in-law did."

Ivan Boesky didn't balk at the price. Gertrude Marks died a year after her brother, and her son, Royal, a concert pianist-turned-art dealer, then controlled the swing points. Whatever price Royal asked for them, Boesky, unbeknownst to the Slatkins, paid without question. With that 4 percent, plus Seema's 48, Ivan Boesky, in an intrafamily coup, became in 1980 the principal stockholder in the Beverly Hills Hotel. It was a sweet revenge for him.

Muriel Slatkin's explanation of why Royal Marks sold the swing points to Ivan Boesky rather than to Burt Slatkin was that there had been bad blood between her father and Royal Marks, and Burt had had to serve as intermediary between the two.

In the most recent *Forbes* magazine list of the four hundred richest people in the United States, Boesky's personal fortune was given as $150 million—more money than Ben Silberstein ever had. Boesky is said to have grossed about $50 million on the 1984 acquisition of Getty Oil by Texaco, and later that year he grossed about $65 million on the acquisition of Gulf Oil by the Standard Oil Company of California. The Boeskys now own a large estate in Westchester County, New York, as well as an apartment in Paris. Seema Boesky is often seen at sales of Impressionist paintings at Sotheby's, bidding and buying, and there are Renoirs on her walls.

After Boesky's takeover in 1981, the Slatkins waited for the other shoe to drop. Meanwhile, their marriage fell apart. Muriel continues to live in the Regency mansion, but Burt now lives elsewhere. Muriel has a boyfriend, a Chilean named Ricardo Pascal. Pascal is younger than Muriel, and the relationship has caused tension between Muriel and her two boys. When one of the sons, Tommy, got married last July, there was public controversy over whether or not he had invited his mother to the wedding ceremony. She made an appearance at the reception.

Burt Slatkin continued as president of the hotel and oversaw all building and refurbishing of the bungalows on the grounds. He also continued to handle routine management problems, such as that presented by the aging and ailing Norton Simon, the multimillionaire industrialist and art collector, who for a time lived in one of the bungalows. Simon took to appearing in the Polo Lounge for breakfast wearing pajamas, a bathrobe, and slippers, and no one on the staff had the nerve to challenge him. Finally Slatkin made a discreet appeal to Simon's wife, the former film star Jennifer Jones, suggesting that her husband's attire in the public rooms of the hotel might encourage other guests to follow suit.

Ivan Boesky held the controlling interest in the hotel for almost five years before he made his move. Opinions differ as to why, after waiting so long, he struck when he did—pulling the rug out from under his sister-in-law, Muriel Slatkin.

"She said something to Seema about Ivan that went too far, and Ivan retaliated," said one observer.

Another explanation was that she called him a moron once too often at the counter of the coffee shop.

Whatever, it happened. In July 1985, Ivan Boesky arrived in Beverly Hills and checked in at his regular suite, 135–36, which had been redecorated to his specifications and which was rented or lent to his friends when he was not there. He called a meeting of all employees, from executives to bellboys, even those on their day off, in the Crystal Room, the principal ballroom of the hotel. There he announced to the startled staff that from that moment on the president and chief executive officer of the hotel was no longer Burton Slatkin but Adalberto M. Stratta, president of Princess Hotels International when it was owned by D. K. Ludwig. Slatkin was given the title of chairman of the board, but the implication was clear to all: Boesky's man, Stratta, was now the man in charge.

Muriel Slatkin was stripped of all her perks. Her office in the hotel was taken away, and she was informed that she was no longer welcome in any capacity other than guest, with the same privileges as any other paying guest. Her double cabana at the pool was confiscated, although she could rent it by the day if she called and it had not already been booked. Her favorite table in the Polo Lounge was no longer hers to command. Her charges in the drugstore were no longer to be paid by the hotel. "She was so embarrassed she didn't dare walk through the lobby," said one of her friends. Muriel Slatkin without the Beverly Hills Hotel was like King Zog without Albania. Shamed by her treatment and inconsolable, she took to her bed and saw no one, except Ricardo Pascal and a few close friends, for six weeks.

Now a family showdown is brewing. Muriel, recovered, and Burt, from whom she is not divorced, have jointly hired the Washington, D.C., law firm of Edward Bennett Williams to protect their interests. And Ivan Boesky has poured a fortune into the hotel, amid rumors of a sale. Seema Boesky declined to be interviewed for this article and declined for her husband as well.

"Could you just tell me about the four percent, Mrs. Boesky, whether your husband . . ."

"Do your own research," replied Seema Boesky.

I called Muriel Slatkin in Beverly Hills to ask her if she would see me if I flew out. She was undecided. "I love my sister. I don't understand why she is doing this to me," she said. "She is humiliating me. She has taken away everything. I don't even get a ten percent discount anymore." Reflecting on their childhood, she said, "My sister was heavy and not as popular as me. I'm not going to become bitter about it. My sister is the culprit. She wants to annihilate me."

I flew to Beverly Hills and checked in at the Beverly Hills Hotel. Grant Tinker, chairman of NBC, was making a telephone call in the lobby. Alan Ladd, Jr., the president of MGM/UA, strolled through with Guy McElwaine, the chairman of Columbia Pictures, and Barry Diller, the chairman of Twentieth Century-Fox, rushed past on his way to a meeting. In my room I found a bouquet of flowers, a bottle of wine, a basket of fruit, and a personal note of welcome from Burton Slatkin, chairman of the board. The telephone operator called me by name on my first call. In spite of everything, the Beverly Hills Hotel was still the Beverly Hills Hotel.

"Can you have lunch today?" I asked Muriel Slatkin when the hotel operator put me through to her house.

"No, I'm having lunch at the Bistro Garden with my boyfriend," she replied.

"Tomorrow?"

"I have houseguests for the weekend."

"When?"

"Monday tea?"

"Fine."

"Three o'clock in the Polo Lounge," she said. Later she changed it to three o'clock at her house. Later still she cancelled altogether. "Eddie Bennett Williams said under no condition can I talk to you," she said.

Since Seema wouldn't talk, and Muriel was now silenced, I turned to their cousin Royal Marks, who by selling his 4 percent had started the war. When I called him at his art gallery in New York and identified myself by name and magazine, he replied, "I'm not interested in a subscription."

Lazarama

"I'M TRYING to find Janet de Cordova."

"She's seated in that corner between Tom Selleck and Johnny Carson. At the table next to Jimmy Stewart's."

"I feel like I'm going to be trampled to death by movie stars."

"Nobody but Swifty could get all these people under one roof. Nobody."

When Mrs. William Backhouse Astor, Jr., built her vast Fifth Avenue mansion in 1857, she had the ballroom designed to dance four hundred guests, and for her first ball she called on the social arbiter of that time, Ward McAllister, to draw up a list of New York's four hundred grandest people. There was much jockeying for McAllister's favor, as well as gnashing of teeth by those not invited, and from then on society itself became known as the Four Hundred.

In recent years, in Hollywood of all places, an unlikely successor to Ward McAllister has emerged in the person of Irving Paul Lazar, the diminutive septuagenarian agent, known far and wide as Swifty. The Academy Awards party he and his wife, Mary, have hosted for twenty-five years has become *the* place to be, and his guest list, as carefully honed as Ward McAllister's, varies each year as people gain or lose prominence. On Lazar's list, success has replaced McAllister's criterion of pedigree. "Are you going to Swifty's?" people in Hollywood ask weeks in advance. Immense pressure is brought to bear on both Lazars by people who have not been invited, but Swifty has not got to the top of the heap in

Hollywood and remained there for almost four decades by being a softy. "NO!" is the answer people say he gives. Or, if the person calling, or being called about, interests him, the answer is "Come after dinner." Sometimes he even qualifies that by adding, "Late!"

Although Spago, the trendy West Hollywood restaurant where the party has been given for the last two years, is smaller than Mrs. Astor's ballroom nearly the same number of people crossed its threshold during the three waves of this year's nine-hour party. In the first wave were 190 members of the Hollywood establishment and a few billionaires. In the after-dinner crowd were people who had attended the ceremony but bypassed the Academy's Governor's Ball. In the third wave came those who had also gone to the ball. All evening Swifty moved through the rooms like a ringmaster, directing traffic, telling people to get back in their seats.

"I can't see anything," complained one man. "I mean, it's hard to say to Raquel Welch, 'Hey, Raquel, you're blocking the TV.' " "I'd like to be a fly on that table where Jessica Lange, Meryl Streep, Kathleen Turner, and Sally Field have their heads together," said his friend.

Audrey Hepburn, who had presented an Oscar, arrived late to a standing ovation.

"Audrey!" cried Elizabeth Taylor.

"Elizabeth!" cried Audrey Hepburn, leaning over a table to kiss her.

"Ouch! You stepped on my toe!" yelped Elizabeth Taylor to a passerby.

"Oh, God, William Hurt brought the whole *Spider Woman* crowd with him," said Mary Lazar.

"Where are Jack and Anjelica?"

"They had to go to that damn ball."

The Mortimer's Bunch

MORTIMER'S, the restaurant on the corner of Lexington Avenue and Seventy-fifth Street, is the best show in New York. If you can get a table. But don't count on getting a table. Far less well known to the general public than fancy places like Le Cirque, the Four Seasons, or Lutèce, where the concentration is on *grande cuisine*, Mortimer's is all about ambience. On any given day you are likely to see, at lunch or dinner, alone or in combination, Jacqueline Onassis, Ahmet Ertegun, Brooke Astor, Bobby Short, Peter Duchin, Marietta Tree, Fran Lebowitz, Placido Domingo, William S. Paley, Valerian Rybar, Katherine Graham, Mark Hampton, Mariel Hemingway, Oscar de la Renta, Mike Wallace, Patricia Kennedy Lawford, Jean Kennedy Smith, Lord Snowdon, Yasmin Khan, Marsha Mason, C. Z. Guest, Greta Garbo, Jean Vanderbilt, Jeanne Vanderbilt, Gloria Vanderbilt. The A list goes on and on.

Gloria Vanderbilt says Mortimer's is like Rick's Café in *Casablanca*, with Glenn Bernbaum, the owner, in the Humphrey Bogart role. "The things that go on there!" she exclaims. "And, you know, he lives upstairs in that incredible place. There's nothing like it in New York."

"I think Glenn Bernbaum is one of the most charming hosts that I've ever encountered in any establishment," says the record mogul Ahmet Ertegun. "He's low-key. He's elegant. He's a gentleman. His place has become—along with Elaine's—the other meeting place."

Irving Lazar, the Hollywood literary agent and social martinet, says that "Glennbaum," as he calls him, has "a genius for seating."

One afternoon recently, arriving at Mortimer's to have a late lunch with Bernbaum, I found him in a grumpy mood. The computer service that prepares the payroll for his staff of sixty had made the checks out on the wrong bank, and the error had definitely put him out of sorts. He was wearing a tweed jacket, an ecru custom-made shirt, gray flannels, and, surprisingly, Top-Siders. His clothes are beautifully cut and tailored, the kind that last forever. His hair is trimmed short, in the Ivy League style, and he wears horn-rimmed glasses with brown tinted lenses. He is sixty-one years old.

"You missed a good lunch," he said, when he had finally calmed down. He was not referring to the food but to the cast list of the day, and he began reeling off the names of some of the people, at the same time pointing out by number the tables where he had seated them.

Bernbaum will deny to you that the restaurant is snobbish, but make no mistake about it: it is. "We don't take reservations," you are told when you phone to book a table, "except for parties of five or more." And when you arrive to take your chances, the eyes of the captain at the door can be as unwelcoming as if you had walked into the sacrosanct halls of the Knickerbocker Club or the Brook Club without being a member. Yet there always seem to be tables for the high-profile names of New York. "Well," conceded Bernbaum when I asked him about this, "we don't take reservations, but we do, of course, take care of our friends." Behind his glasses, his eyes retreated into thought about what he had said, and he qualified his remark. "On the other hand, if I see someone who's an attractive person, the kind we want in the restaurant, with inherent style, there's always a place for that kind of person." He thought again and added, "If liking people with style is being a snob, then I'm a snob, I suppose."

Michael Connolly, one of the two waiters called Michael

who handle the celebrity section during lunch, paused with a tray on which was a tin of beluga caviar that Bernbaum was sending to the table where Mercedes Kellogg, the wife of Ambassador Francis Kellogg, was giving a birthday lunch for two to Hubert de Givenchy, the French couturier.

"Does this look all right?" asked Connolly.

"Hmmmm," replied Bernbaum, examining the tray. He changed the position of a lemon wedge.

"Should there be watercress on the tray?" asked Michael.

"Good God, no, and that spoon's all wrong. Get a bigger spoon." Bernbaum added, "If you're going to do it, do it right." It is one of the rules he lives by.

Bernbaum grew up in private splendor in Philadelphia. A World War II army friend, Boy Scheftel, who knew him when he was a lieutenant in psychological warfare, describes the Bernbaum wealth as "Philadelphia money and a lot of it." Before starting Mortimer's in 1976, Bernbaum had achieved success as executive vice president of the Custom Shop Shirt-makers.

In Bernbaum's stylish apartment upstairs over the restaurant, there is a drawing of his family's town house on Delancey Place in Philadelphia. The apartment is one open effect of a vast room in an exotic country house. There are lacquered cabinets, paintings of Turkish sultans, a French desk, and sofas covered with fur throws. Over the fireplace hangs a portrait of his late mother, with hands on hips, dark hair cut in bangs, wearing black velvet and pearls, and looking almost exactly like Vita Sackville-West. There's a photograph in a silver frame of his mother and her great friend, the opera star Lily Pons, and another of the first lady, Nancy Reagan, in an affectionate pose with her adjutant, Jerry Zipkin. Over one of the sofas is an eighteenth-century painting of a hound attacking a felled stag.

"It's a Baldassare de Caro," said Bernbaum, looking up at it. Then he added, "Maybe," and smiled.

When Bernbaum opened Mortimer's ten years ago, he

knew nothing about running a restaurant. Two friends, Bill Blass and Steve Kaufmann, brought him together with Michael Pearman, who had created such famous New York establishments as Michael's Pub and the Running Footman. "He didn't know where to get coffee, or meat, or how to hire staff," said Pearman, from Palm Beach, where he now lives. Bernbaum concedes that Pearman got his backers to frequent Mortimer's (which was named after Mortimer Levitt, who owns the Custom Shop Shirtmakers), but adds, "I also knew a few people quite well: Bill Blass, Kenny Lane, and Jerry Zipkin. They were immediate boosters of the restaurant. Of course, we can't detract from the location. Everyone lives close by."

"There are two cardinal rules in the restaurant business," said Pearman. "Never take a drink in front of the staff, and never, ever, sit down with a customer, no matter how well you know them. Glenn does both these things."

"Pearman wanted the restaurant to reflect his personality, and I wanted it to reflect mine," said Bernbaum.

The arrangement between the two did not work out, so Pearman withdrew and returned to Palm Beach. Sometime later he dined in the restaurant with a friend and complained that his chicken paillard was protruding over the edge of the plate. Meant constructively, the criticism was resented by Bernbaum, and he walked off without replying. Pearman has not visited the restaurant since.

Bernbaum is sensitive to any criticism of the food he serves. Jerry Zipkin and he temporarily fell out over Zipkin's criticism of the spinach. Zipkin claimed, according to Bernbaum, that the spinach was always creamed. Why couldn't the restaurant serve leaf spinach? Bernbaum replied tartly that creamed spinach had to be leaf spinach before it became creamed spinach, and if Zipkin wanted leaf spinach he should ask for it. Except for private parties, the fare at Mortimer's is simple—crab cakes, twinburgers, chicken paillard, and fresh fish—and the prices are remarkably cheap for so tony an establishment.

There are other rifts. A current one is with Kenneth Jay Lane, the jewelry designer and man-about-town, whom many people credit with the enormous success of the restaurant. The art historian John Richardson says, "As Pratt's Club in London caters to the personal friends of the Duke of Devonshire, so Mortimer's in New York caters to the personal friends of Kenny Lane."

"Tell me about Glenn," I asked Kenny Lane when I ran across him at the Morgan Library looking at drawings from the Albertina.

"The social arbiter?" he replied, eyebrows raised, a note of irony in his voice. Bernbaum had been so described in a recent magazine interview. "I seem to have been dropped by Mr. Bernbaum. However, I'm delighted that the restaurant is doing so well that I can no longer get a reservation there."

Their rift was over seating. According to Bernbaum, Lane was displeased with the table he was shown to, and simply moved his party of four to a better one, which was reserved for someone else. Bernbaum was annoyed.

Bernbaum is a complicated man, paradoxically rude and kind, distant and warm, sad and funny. He is invariably well informed on the comings and goings of other people. "Mrs. Reagan is having lunch at Mrs. Buckley's today," he will tell you. Or "Oona Chaplin's apartment burned and she's moved to the Carlyle." Or "I hear Princess Margaret's smoking like a chimney, and after that lung operation."

Bernbaum has not been without his own share of gossip and melodrama. While vacationing on the island of Crete in 1975, he was so impressed by a waiter called Stefanos that he asked him to move to New York and work at Mortimer's. It then developed that Stefanos had a wife and child, and Bernbaum agreed to move them to New York too. He made Stefanos a captain, and the young man's charm ingratiated him with the regulars of the establishment. But Stefanos gambled, and soon he was heavily in debt to the kind of people who break your legs if you can't pay. Bernbaum, in the meantime, had made out a new will, leaving Mortimer's to Stefanos, and he told Stefanos that he would be his heir. Impatient to pay off the underworld figures, who were after him, Stefanos sought to hurry along the inheritance process by contracting two hit men to do away with his benefactor. His plan was discovered, and the two hit men who arrived at the restaurant turned out to be F.B.I. agents. Stefanos was arrested on the spot, tried, and sent to the slammer.

The incident was reported in the press, and Taki Theodoracopulos wrote about it in graphic detail in the pages of the *Spectator*. Such is the level of sophistication at Mortimer's, however, that when Taki's book *Princes, Playboys, & High-Class Tarts*, which includes the piece on Bernbaum and the Greek waiter, appeared, Bernbaum gave the publication party at the restaurant, because it was Taki's favorite New York hangout.

Bernbaum is famous for the private parties he arranges at Mortimer's. Several years after opening the restaurant, he expanded into the building next door and turned the new space into a second dining room, suitable for private parties. Last year he expanded further by adding the Café Mortimer around the corner on Seventy-fifth Street; it serves sandwiches and pizza and also functions as a room for small parties.

"I gave the first party at Mortimer's," Kenny Lane told me. "One hundred of the A list in twelve different languages. Glenn provided the food, and I provided the people. The guests never left. They're still there."

I arrived one afternoon to find Bernbaum arranging white lilacs and pink roses in small glass vases for a private party that evening. He treats each party as if he were the host, and he proudly displays albums filled with color photographs of Cornelia Guest's coming-out party, Bill Blass and Oscar de la Renta's party for the publication of Diana Vreeland's book *D.V.*, opera patron Sybil Harrington's birthday party for Placido Domingo, and the 1984 red-white-and-blue, election-night party hosted by the Ahmet Erteguns, the Irving Lazars, and the Abraham Ribicoffs.

Joel Gerbino, one of the three maîtres d'hotel, rushed into the restaurant and delivered six swatches of Liberty of London prints to his employer. The following night the American-born Lady Keith, known as Slim in the circles in which she travels, was giving a dinner for twenty in honor of her daughter, Kitty Hawks (from her marriage to the late Howard Hawks), her stepdaughter Brooke Hayward (from her marriage to the late producer Leland Hayward), and her stepdaughter Lady Camilla Mackeson (from her marriage to Lord Keith). Bernbaum wanted to make the evening special, and he fussed over which of the six fabrics would make the proper tablecloths for Lady Keith's party. Invariably he adds extra touches at his own expense if he feels they will make the evening exceptional. He rapidly figured on a piece of paper that each tablecloth would come to $250. "I hate to spend that much money and not get something I really like," he said. "I can't very well charge Slim Keith for print tablecloths from Liberty of London that she didn't order, but I'll be able to use the tablecloths again, and isn't it more important to get it done right?" He looked out the window and patted the back of his head.

"No one but a nut would agonize like this over a dinner for twenty."

By party time the next evening the Café Mortimer looked as if it were ready for a children's party, a rich children's party, which is what it was, even though the children were all grown-up and divorced themselves. Helium balloons with silver lamé streamers hugged the ceiling. The centerpieces were large jars of candy, and *Wind in the Willows* beanbag animals anchored the place cards on the candlelit tables, which were covered with Liberty of London tablecloths rushed to completion for $250 apiece. "Dim the lights so we can see how it's going to look," Bernbaum said to Michael Connolly. He crossed his arms and stared up at the balloons. "Give me a scissors," he said. "These ribbons are too long."

•   •   •

"Taste this Tofu that Gloria Vanderbilt sent over this morning," said Bernbaum to his chef, Stephen Attoe, formerly of the Connaught Hotel in London. Tofu dessert is the latest product carrying the illustrious Vanderbilt name. "I must say I never saw ice cream delivered so beautifully," he went on. "Her own car. Her own driver. Gloria's got style. What do you think of it?"

Stephen Attoe sampled the three flavors and liked them all.

"Reinaldo Herrera gave a lunch at Le Cirque for Princess Margaret yesterday," Bernbaum said to his chef. "It would have been here if the *poisson* had been cooked properly the other night when Reinaldo came in for dinner. It was underdone, he said." There was a slight reprimand in his voice.

He likes royalty and apparently royalty likes Mortimer's. On one of the Princess Margaret's visits to New York, she was entertained at the River Café in a small party that included Jack and Drue Heinz, of the pickle-and-ketchup Heinzes, and Bill Blass. A ripple of excitement ran through the restaurant as the elegant party made its way to the table. "There's Bill Blass," the celebrity watchers whispered, while Her Royal Highness went virtually unrecognized. She was not pleased. The following night the princess was given a large party at Mortimer's by the Venezuelan socialite and landowner Reinaldo Herrera and his dress-designer wife, Carolina. Glenn Bernbaum, who had heard the story of the River Café, instructed the piano player to play "There'll Always Be an England," and "Rule Britannia," and he prompted the diners in the main room to stand and applaud the queen's sister. As the princess was leaving the party, she informed Bernbaum that he had given her her most pleasant evening in New York.

Another night, the king and queen of Spain entertained in the restaurant. Bernbaum was determined to keep their evening at Mortimer's private. "No one knew he was coming," said Bernbaum.

"Not even the staff. I put the family name on the reservation list."

"What is the family name?"

"It's slipped my mind for a minute, but I'll look it up for you."

He did. It was Bourbon.

"They had the window table in the second room. I seated the king at the head of the table with his back to the window. The security people had a fit. Because of the Basque separatists. How was I to know the Basque separatists were out to get him? Well, Pierre Cardin was also having a dinner in the restaurant the same night, for the same number of people, and I thought of swapping tables, but I left the king at the window table. I just moved his seat so the head of the table was against the brick wall. The next day the embassy in Washington called to say that this was the only place in New York where there weren't TV cameras. I even assigned the waiter who always waits on Garbo to the king's table."

One night, quite late, three men entered the restaurant, pulled guns, and told the remaining diners to lie on the floor while they emptied the cash register. "Thank God the Aga Kahn and Sally had just left," said Bernbaum.

It *is* Rick's Café, and he does have a genius for seating. Claus von Bülow, shortly before his second trial for the attempted murder of his wife, the utilities heiress Martha "Sunny" Crawford von Bülow, was lunching one day in Mortimer's with Grace, Countess of Dudley, and John Richardson. Directly behind von Bülow, Bernbaum seated Arthur Schlesinger and Lally Weymouth, the daughter of Katherine Graham, the owner of the *Washington Post,* even though Mrs. Weymouth had written a series of articles unfavorable to von Bülow at the time of his first trial.

Von Bülow maintained his high profile in New York between trials by lunching at Mortimer's several days a week, usually with his girlfriend, Andrea Reynolds. He always entered the restaurant like a film star. His detractors, and there are many, voiced disapproval at his presence there; his supporters, and there are many, greeted and joked with him.

Bernbaum performed a delicate balancing act whenever von Bülow's stepchildren, Alexander von Auersperg and his sister Ala von Auersperg Kneissl, who believe him guilty of having attempted to murder their mother, were in the restaurant at the same time as von Bülow. Bernbaum always seated them at a distance from each other so that no unfortunate incidents could occur.

The von Bülow presence at Mortimer's was not a subject that Bernbaum wanted to talk about, but it was unavoidable. He is too good a restaurateur to be unmindful of the theatrical effect von Bülow had on other customers.

"I never showed him off," said Bernbaum. He weighed his words carefully. "His stepchildren no longer come here," he said. "Claus has never been anything other than a gent. I don't think it's up to me to pass judgment on him. If anybody didn't act properly, that would be another story."

"Have you ever barred anyone from the restaurant?"

"Several people."

"Why?"

"Unpleasant. Ungentlemanly. Unladylike."

"Who?"

He smiled, shrugged, and didn't reply.

Michael Ludwig, the other waiter called Michael, came over and asked, "Do you want to give a reservation for Sunday lunch to Harrison Goldin?"

"Who's Harrison Goldin?" asked Bernbaum.

"The comptroller of the City of New York," replied Michael. Neither of them seemed impressed.

Bernbaum looked out the window for a moment, patted the back of his head, looked back at Michael, and replied, "Oh, give it to him."

The Women of Palm Beach

PALM BEACH people talk about Palm Beach people constantly. It is a subject that never seems to exhaust itself, and any one of them, at any event where they are gathered, can give you an instant precis of any other one's life. "She's Mollie Netcher Bragno Bostwick Wilmot. She lives next to Rose Kennedy, and last year a tanker ran aground on her seawall and practically landed in her living room." . . . "The man in the receiving line, third from the end, is Paul Hynsky. He's on the town council. His father was a Russian grand duke who married Audrey Emery, Paul's mother, and his second cousin was the last czar of Russia." . . . "The lady with the long blonde hair who never misses a dance is Sue Whitmore, the Listerine heiress. She was practically born at the old Royal Poinciana Hotel. She single-handedly runs the International Red Cross Ball every year, which is the only one of the big charity parties the chic people go to." . . . "There, with the deep tan and the mustache, is Douglas Fairbanks, Jr. I don't have to tell you who he is, except that his house, for some reason, is called the Vicarage." . . . "That elderly lady being helped across the dance floor by Charlie Van Rensselaer is Mary Sanford, Laddie Sanford's widow—you know, the polo player. They call her the Queen of Palm Beach. Don't say I called her elderly." . . . "The guy with the pale pink lipstick and the plucked eyebrows and the big diamond ring in the color photograph in the window of Kohn's on Worth Avenue is Arndt Krupp, the German munitions heir. Last year he gave a big party for the Queen of Thailand, but nobody's seen him this year." . . . "She's Lilly

McKim Pulitzer Rousseau. Everybody loves Lilly. She's Ogden
Phipps's stepdaughter, and she used to be married to Peter
Pulitzer, years before all that awful Roxanne business, and
they were the most beautiful couple in Palm Beach. Now she's
married to Enrique Rousseau, one of the Cubans, and Enrique's ex-wife is now married to Charlie Amory, who used to
be married to Chessy Patcevitch. I hope you can keep all this
straight." . . . "That's Bill Ylvisaker. He's the polo group.
Sundays everyone goes to Wellington for the polo." . . .
"The tall man sitting next to Estée Lauder is Joe Sobotka.
He's one of the better extra men down here. Sometimes you
have to scrape the bottom of the barrel for good extra men
for these parties." . . . "The beautiful redhead in the gold
dress is Fern Tailer Gimble Denney, Tommy Tailer's daughter, Edith Baker's granddaughter, and the man she's talking
to is Alfonso Fanjul. One of the Cubans. Sugar money. Rich,
rich, rich." . . . "At the next table, in the T-shirt, carrying
her gardening book, is C. Z. Guest, Mrs. Winston Guest, the
famous gardener. She's become rather independent down
here. And sitting next to her, in the black bathing suit with
the long blonde hair, is her daughter, Cornelia, who's always
in the papers." . . . "There's Suzie Phipps, perfectly beautiful
and sitting on twenty-six acres in the middle of Palm Beach.
She, I suppose, is the real Palm Beach." . . . "That's Dorothy
Spreckels Munn. She lives in an Addison Mizner-style house
on what was the Munn compound with ten indoor servants.
You can't get any higher than Dorothy Munn and the
Phippses in Palm Beach."

"Everybody who ever writes about Palm Beach always gets
it wrong," said a very grand lady to me during a lunch party
on my first day there. She stared down at the silver platter of
gnocchi that was being served to her, shook her head no to
the maid, changed her mind, and took a minuscule portion.
"They come down here, these writers, stay too short a time,
don't get to the Bath and Tennis Club or the Everglades,
never meet anyone, except all those old dragons who love

publicity and aren't Palm Beach at all, and then they go back to wherever they're from and think they're authorities on Palm Beach and write the most awful things about us. Did you ever see that English television show they did? I mean, really. None of us even knew who those grotesques were they interviewed for that show. And it's always like that. Not one person was Real Palm Beach."

Just who is and who isn't "real Palm Beach" is a recurring theme in Palm Beach conversations. The grand lady, her morsel of gnocchi consumed, lit a cigarette and threw back her head as she exhaled, as if to stress how the journalistic portrayals of her winter resort annoyed her. She was tanned and slender and pretty, wore a print silk dress, pearls, and a straw hat, and would, when this lunch was over, play bridge until dinner. "The trouble is," she continued, "that everyone thinks Roxanne Pulitzer is Palm Beach." She pronounced the name Roxanne Pulitzer with an intonation that let you know in no uncertain terms exactly what she thought of that person, which wasn't much. "She's not Palm Beach, and never was, and none of us ever saw Roxanne and Peter, even before that horrible divorce. They were always with the Kimberlys, and that's a different group entirely. And as for Mr. Armand Hammer! Puhleeze!"

Mr. Armand Hammer, the chairman of the board of Occidental Petroleum, won the eternal enmity of most of the real Palm Beach for his high-handed treatment of them when he presided over a charity ball during the visit of Prince Charles and Princess Diana to the resort in November 1985. The real Palm Beach boycotted the affair.

The grand lady stared down at the dessert plate that had been placed in front of her by the maid, lifted off the spoon and fork, and transferred the finger bowl and doily from the plate to the table. "You see," she went on, "Palm Beach, I mean the real Palm Beach, is behind walls, and very private, and that's why none of you people who come down here to write about it ever get it right."

The lush and lovely Florida island, which faces the Atlantic Ocean on one side and Lake Worth on the other, is the winter counterpart of such northern summer resorts as Newport, Southampton, and Bar Harbor. It is only twelve miles long. Here rich people can enjoy being rich without fear of criticism, because almost no one lives in Palm Beach except other rich people enjoying being rich. During the sixties and seventies, some of the Old Guard, fearing that Palm Beach had seen better days, abandoned it and took or built houses in Acapulco or on smart Caribbean islands like Jamaica, but the unsightly poverty, "the racial thing," and the fear of uprisings brought them back to where their eyes need only look upon other people living exactly as they are living, in large and lovely pastel-colored villas with well-tended lawns and hedges and well-trained staffs to manage them. But even here, in this most rarefied existence of rank and privilege, there is heard a constant lament that things are not as good as they used to be.

It's possible to go to Palm Beach bearing all the right credentials, spend the season in a pretty house or the Colony Hotel or the Breakers, and never lay eyes on any of the people you've heard about, or read about, all your life, who are, as the saying goes, the real Palm Beach. But they're there, behind their walls, just as the grand lady said to me, and their social life, for those of them who like social life, is relentless. There are lunch parties and cocktail parties and dinner parties, and a great deal of stopping by friends' houses for drinks on the way to the parties or on the way home from the parties. And there are charity balls, although there is a hierarchy of charity balls, and this group attends only the three or four where the guest list is limited to "people we know." In between the parties, the same people see one another at the Bath and Tennis Club, called the B. and T. by its members, or the Everglades Club, for lunch, or dinner, or tennis, or croquet, or golf, or a swim. They are mostly dressed alike, the men in lemon or lime or raspberry linen trousers with blue blazers and loafers without socks, and the women in very understated beach or golf wear, except for the group that plays bridge every afternoon, who are slightly dressier.

Exclusivity is the name of the game in the real Palm Beach: being with your own kind and your own kind's houseguests, excluding, for the most part, all others. To be asked to join the two clubs that count; to be invited to the Coconuts on New Year's Eve, the most in of the in New Year's Eve parties, with its receiving line of twenty men; to be invited to buy tickets for the Planned Parenthood and the Community Foundation dinner dances and the Preservation Foundation Ball—these are all signs that you're accepted, or that you've made it. But unless your name appears on one of the two overlapping lists of under three hundred names with unlisted telephone numbers that are sent out each year, like mini-social registers, one in the form of a Christmas card by the enormously rich Fanjul family, the other by the socially prominent realtor Anthony Boalt, you're not really the real Palm Beach. "People are dying to get on those lists," one lady told me in the snobbese characteristic of people who believe that inherited wealth is superior to earned wealth, "but, you know, there are some business people on them now. When Charlie Munn used to do the list every year, there were only social people on it."

In the swell houses on South Ocean Boulevard the living is indeed very swell and being shown through the cool and elegant rooms and the grounds on a sort of privately conducted tour by the owner is part of each visit. In one, a butler in a well-tailored white jacket and white gloves stood at the end of a chintz-upholstered drawing room, a presence but not a participant, waiting to replenish drinks and hors d'oeuvres while we talked. On the wall hung, as there hangs on the wall of almost every fashionable house here, a portrait of the lady of the house painted by Alejo Vidal-Quadras, the resident Boldini of Palm Beach.

"Need I tell you what people talk about in resorts?" asked my hostess of that day, reclining on a sofa beneath her Vidal-Quadras portrait. " 'The gardener didn't come.' 'I hate my new maid.' 'Who did you sit next to at Chessy's last night?' I mean, it goes like that, day in, day out."

She has been coming to Palm Beach most of her life, as has her mother, who lives nearby. She sipped her Perrier water, declined an hors d'oeuvre with a shake of her head to the butler, and petted a King Charles spaniel that had jumped up on the sofa next to her. Like everyone else, she lamented that Palm Beach was not the way it used to be. "It's too bad about all those other people coming to Palm Beach," she said, lowering her voice, although she was in her own drawing room, "you know, the fifty percent, but we never have to see them. That's what's so wonderful about the clubs. You can't even bring them there as a guest. You'd get a little letter in the mail if you did, and then, if you did it again, bye-bye membership in the Bath and Tennis."

"Those other people," the 50 percent she was talking about, referred to what is most commonly called "the Jewish thing," about which no one likes to commit himself, although it is a constant in conversation. One man told me, "Palm Beach is the only unabashedly Wasp community left in the United States, but we're up-front about it." Other people consider Palm Beach a bastion of anti-Semitism. Because the Bath and Tennis and the Everglades clubs are restricted, the rich Jews of Palm Beach are ineligible for membership. As David Marcus of the *Miami Herald* wrote last year, in a series of articles on the private clubs which incensed many of the Old Guard, "No matter how wealthy, how prominent or how impeccable their credentials, Jews are not welcome at these exclusive social institutions." The feeling is that this sort of thing is better left unsaid.

What makes the matter a constant source of beneath-the-surface acrimony is the so-called guest rule, and members of both clubs are divided in their feelings about it. While it nowhere states in the rules that Jews, blacks, or other ethnic minorities cannot come as guests of members, the guest rule at the Everglades states that members may not bring anyone they "might reasonably believe would not be accepted as a member." Quite simply, this means that these clubs will not even permit a Jew to walk through the door as the guest of a member.

There are endless stories of acutely embarrassing situations that have occurred when people have brought Jewish friends to the clubs and the friends have been asked to leave the golf course, or the tennis courts, or the dining room. In one particularly irksome case, the head of the Palm Beach branch of an international company cannot bring the chairman of the board of the company to his clubs, even though the chairman of the board is a winter resident of Palm Beach.

The Everglades Club was built in 1917 on 160 acres of prime real estate by Addison Mizner, the architect who developed the Palm Beach style, a rococo olio of Moorish, Spanish, and Italianate elements. Originally conceived as a convalescent home for mentally disturbed servicemen by the multimillionaire Paris Singer, a lover of Isadora Duncan and one of the twenty-five children of Isaac Merritt Singer, the sewing-machine magnate, it was converted into a private social club two years later. An oil portrait of Paris Singer hangs inside the double doors, past the MEMBERS ONLY sign. Although it was Singer who restricted the membership of the club, Palm Beach legend has it that he himself was suspected of being Jewish. Herbert Bayard Swope, Jr., a radio and television commentator and a member of the croquet set, says, "On that rumor alone, Paris Singer wouldn't get into the club to see his own portrait today."

A mile down the road is the Bath and Tennis Club, facing the Atlantic. It was built in 1926 in the Mizner tradition.

In the 1950s the Jews founded their own club, the Palm Beach Country Club, where the initiation fee is reputed to be $50,000, higher than the initiation fee at either the Everglades or the Bath and Tennis, and the annual dues are $4,000. Eligibility for membership in this club is unique in

that it has to do more with an applicant's recognized involvement with charitable contributions than with social standing,
good schools, and the right connections. Members of the
Palm Beach Country Club can bring Christians as guests,
although there is only one Christian, Phil O'Connell, Sr.,
among the 325 members.

At the turn of the century, when the first great hotels like
the Royal Poinciana and the Breakers were being built to lure
the New York and Newport aristocracy to the new winter
paradise, there developed nearby, on what is today condo-
minium-lined Sunrise Avenue, a shantytown known as the
Styx, inhabited by the blacks who were brought in to build
the hotels. According to local lore, the unsightly community
offended the eye of Henry Flagler, known as the founder of
Palm Beach, and other town fathers. In a magnanimous-ap-
pearing gesture, they invited the entire population of the Styx
over to West Palm Beach to a circus performance and barbe-
cue, and during their absence burned the shantytown to the
ground. The workers were relocated permanently in West
Palm Beach.

"Money talks."

"Honey, money shrieks."

The two ladies were discussing the imminent arrival on the
Palm Beach scene of two of the most successful young businessmen in America, Leslie Wexner and Donald Trump. Last
season Wexner, the low-profile head of the Limited and some
2,500 specialty apparel shops, with a personal fortune of $1
billion, was the subject of much speculation when he purchased the magnificent estate of Charles and Jayne Wrights-
man for $10 million as a companion piece to his recently
purchased $6 million house on the Upper East Side of Man-
hattan. Then, in a spectacular, Candy Spelling gesture that
shocked Palm Beach, he razed the famous house to the
ground. He is now in the process of building himself a Ver-
sailles-type mansion. He is unmarried and thus far virtually
unknown in Palm Beach.

In January, Donald Trump, of the real estate fortune, and

his wife, Ivana, purchased for a mere $5 million the 118-room mansion called Mar-a-Lago, former house of the late Marjorie Merriweather Post, which had been on the market for $15 million. Mar-a-Lago was conceived by a Ziegfeld set designer in a melange of architectural styles. The Trumps have hired a Palm Beach decorator and claim they plan to spend several months of the year here. There is, however, a lurking suspicion among a lot of members of the Bath and Tennis Club, which is next door to Mar-a-Lago, that the Trumps have inside knowledge that gambling is returning to Palm Beach, and that they intend to turn Mar-a-Lago into a gambling casino.

"They'll never get into the clubs," says one faction about the Trumps. Another faction isn't so sure. "They'll let him a little bit in," they say. "Earl E. T. Smith is behind them." Earl E. T. Smith is a former ambassador to Cuba, a former mayor of Palm Beach, a onetime husband of a Vanderbilt, and his support is considered as good as you can get. And the Trumps—whom one woman referred to as "the new darlings of Palm Beach"—have made a smart social move to start off their life here: they have offered Mar-a-Lago to the Preservation Foundation of Palm Beach for its annual ball.

The *Palm Beach Daily News* is known affectionately as the Shiny Sheet because it is printed on a superior quality of glossy paper which guarantees that it can be handled without soiling the fingers or staining the white morning linen. A ninety-two-year-old institution, the Shiny Sheet is devoted exclusively to Palm Beach life, both social and everyday. MRS. VINCENT DRADDY SUES FOR DIVORCE was the headline of one recent front-page story, which recounted the details of the latest in Palm Beach's predilection for messy, no-holds-barred divorces. Another read: FOUNDATION DINNER-DANCE LIVES UP TO ITS BILLING. Another HARD CASH GETS TRUMP A BARGAIN, referring to the purchase of Mar-a-Lago. There was a subhead: "Trump Pays Extra for Estate's Furniture."

While the real Palm Beach crowd tend for the most part to

keep their pictures out of the Shiny Sheet and the other five publications covering Palm Beach life, except when they attend charity balls or committee meetings in preparation for the balls, the rest of the out-every-night population is not reluctant at all to pose as often as possible, and some have become bona fide social celebrities, like Mrs. Helen Tuchbreiter, who is a regular first-nighter at the Royal Poinciana Playhouse and the organizer over the past twenty years of twenty-eight charity balls which raised $10 million for assorted good works.

Helen Bernstein, who writes a regular column for the Shiny Sheet, is the wife of the man who built the New York Telephone building and the great-niece of Kate Wollman, who gave the skating rink in Central Park. A kind and witty lady, she is a perceptive observer of Palm Beach social life. "Here everything is sanitized," she said, sitting in the living room of her dramatic house overlooking Lake Worth. "They pick up the garbage five days a week. Everything that's negative, or not so great, is over the bridge in West Palm Beach."

One of her favorite themes is social climbing. About one of the most prominent ladies in the winter colony, she said, "She's so desperate about it. She doesn't take a moment's vacation from it."

"Do social climbers ever make it?" I asked her.

"To Dorothy Munn's house? No. But, on the other hand, they probably don't even know who Dorothy Munn is. No one makes it to the top of the ladder. The successful ones make it about three-quarters of the way. Some fall back from fatigue, but a true social climber doesn't have the sensitivity to know it's only three-quarters of the way. Let me tell you something about social climbing: it's good for the economy. The serious social climbers underwrite the charity balls. The doors are closing in Palm Beach. In a few years, it won't be easy to see anyone."

When the Shiny Sheet reported that Helmut Newton and I were coming to Palm Beach to do an article on the community for *Vanity Fair*, we had a few experiences of our own.

The mother of a postdeb delivered a letter to Helmut at the Breakers, imploring him to moonlight from his *Vanity Fair* assignment to photograph her daughter's cocktail party.

The party, she wrote, "will bring together the town's top Young Socialites in a more natural, typical setting . . . including our friends, the Sargent Shrivers from Washington, D.C. Mrs. S. is Eunice Kennedy, as you know—and all five boys are here, using Mrs. Kennedy's house, of course. They attended [my daughter's] debut two years ago, and are always included amongst her parties. The young Charles Revson (Countess Ancky) too, are coming. Please do come—you'll enjoy yourself immensely, as well as seeing our Miro's. Picasso & Chagall." On a separate page, she added, "We will render payment in American dollars, not F.F."

Another lady called me at the Colony Hotel. "It would be a shame if you don't talk to me," she said. "It would be like coming to Palm Beach without a dinner jacket. I'm sort of an interesting story. My husband invented the milk carton. He was on CBS news on Monday night as one of the great people who passed away this year.

"I was one of the hostesses of Palm Beach for many years. The last people I entertained were the Queen's cousins. I'm sort of an Elsa Maxwell. I have been the chairman of more balls than you can count in the last twenty years. I own the Duchess of Marlborough's house.

"Would you be kind enough to call me Celia *Lipton* Farris. That's the name I'm known under. I was a household name at fifteen in England. Right now I'm recording my new album in Miami."

Palm Beach goes to a lot of people's heads. Although plenty goes on alcoholically and sexually in the upper circles, the real Palm Beachers tend to forgive one another's transgressions. "I always have to do over my phone book each year because of all the divorces," a well-known hostess told me. "Usually you start to hear about the divorces in April, after the season." At one party I attended, the guests were regaled

with hilarious accounts of how a friend of theirs, an outraged
wife, had taped romantic telephone conversations between
her husband and her former maid, whom he had set up in
West Palm Beach. Another tale, told with sadness, concerned a lady whose life had recently nose-dived, after several
divorces, into alcoholism, drug addiction, and unfortunate
liaisons, culminating in a marriage everyone frowned on, followed by her almost immediate death. It is only when social
figures go public in the newspapers with their transgressions
that the others can be, and are, unforgiving.

"Gregg's not allowed in anyone's house" was a line casually
said about Gregg Sherwood Dodge Moran. "Roxanne has
been squeezed out" was another line I heard, about Roxanne
Pulitzer, as if she were a Florida orange. For these two ladies,
and many other, less publicized ones, the paths of Palm Beach
have been rocky. Although Mrs. Dodge and Mrs. Pulitzer
continue to live in the environs of the grand world they once
were a part of, today they are like fallen angels, castoffs, in
the social scheme of things. Their futures are in the hands of
literary agents, paperback publishers, and TV producers if,
but only if, they tell it like it was.

"Do you ever see Gregg Dodge?" I asked a lady who once
worked on ball committees with her.

"Gregg and I don't have the same kind of friends," she
replied.

"Do you ever see Gregg Dodge?" I asked another lady who
once knew her well.

"I saw her at Razook's trying on a full-length mink coat, so
she must have gotten an advance on that miniseries of hers."
She thought for a moment and then added, "No one sees
Gregg Dodge anymore."

I saw Gregg Dodge, and she still looks like Lana Turner,
with whom she once acted in *The Merry Widow.* Gregg was a
little girl from Wisconsin whose real name was Dora Fjelstad.
She became a Miss America contestant and later the Ches-
terfield Girl, at twenty-seven married Horace Dodge, the automobile heir, had a son by him, became his widow after

several months of separation, inherited $13.5 million, married her bodyguard, Danny Moran, who used to be a New York cop, lived in a mansion in Palm Beach, a Fifth Avenue apartment, an estate in Greenwich, Connecticut, a house in the South of France, a country house in Windsor, England, and a yacht, the *Delphine*, 355 feet, which had a crew of fifty-five. She went bankrupt, had all her possessions sold out from under her by court order to pay her creditors, went through more lawsuits than you could count, including one for libel against her onetime best friend, Mary Sanford, the Queen of Palm Beach. She was with Danny Moran in their bedroom when he shot and killed an intruder, and within hearing range when he shot and killed himself. She is currently living in reduced circumstances in Palm Beach with her son, John Dodge, thirty-two, and her small grandson.

She didn't want me to go to her house. She picked the nearby Epicurean Restaurant, where we met for late-afternoon tea for me and vodka martinis for her. "I don't usually wear all this jewelry in the daytime," she said, about her diamond rings and diamond-and-onyx earrings, "but I was being photographed by Helmut Newton." She is pretty, funny, wounded, down but not out. Although she was most recently Mrs. Danny Moran, she calls herself Mrs. Horace E. Dodge again. Her ocean-to-lake estate on South Ocean Boulevard has been sold. John DeLorean now lives in her apartment at 834 Fifth Avenue. Leona and Harry Helmsley now live in her Greenwich, Connecticut, estate. The other places and the yacht are gone too.

She is used to telling her story and tells it well, as if she were pitching it to a producer or an editor. "I buried my second husband and my mother in the same week," she said. "I went through $13.5 million. . . . I know Palm Beach. It's a social battlefield."

"Are you still a member of the clubs?" I asked.

"No," she replied. "No one asked me to resign. I couldn't afford the dues anymore. Now if I joined, I'd have to pay up past dues, which are fifteen or twenty thousand in each club."

"Do you ever hear from any of the people you used to know down here?"

"The women are the generals down here," she replied. "They run everything. The men just become black-tied, silent bystanders. Mary Sanford and I used to run this town socially. Nobody gave a party without checking with us first. Many people in Palm Beach think they're social, but they're just ticket buyers, meeting other ticket buyers. True society in Palm Beach is in the home."

"Do you ever hear from any of the people you used to know down here?" I repeated.

Her eyes filled with tears. We sat for a moment in silence. "I don't choose to see those people," she said. "I haven't wanted to see anyone. I've been recovering my energies."

"Where do you live?" I asked Roxanne Pulitzer.

"Do you know where the mall is?" she replied on the telephone from Inger's Workout in West Palm Beach, where she is now an aerobics instructor.

"No."

She gave me detailed instructions to a neighborhood across the bridge in West Palm Beach, far removed from where she and Peter Pulitzer used to live. "You'll see the house. There's a Porsche in the carport."

What you see first, after the Porsche in the carport, in Roxanne Pulitzer's pleasant house, are two junior-size bicycles belonging to her eight-year-old twin sons, Mac and Zac. And there is Roxanne herself, the scandalous lady of the messiest divorce case in the history of Palm Beach society. After all the stories of cocaine addiction, sexual promiscuity, and lesbianism, I expected her to be defensive, but she isn't. Roxanne, who was married to multimillionaire Herbert "Peter" Pulitzer for seven years, got a measly $50,000 in the divorce settlement.

"I read somewhere you lived in a dump," I said.

"I did right after the divorce, but it wasn't fair for the boys to come from Peter's house to my little place. I got some money when I posed for *Playboy*, so I decided that Mac and Zac and I were going to have a nice place for a year. I'll probably have to move out when the lease is up, unless something happens from the book I'm writing or the miniseries."

"How often do you see your sons?"

"I lost custody of the boys, so I only get to see them four days a month," she said. "And I wasn't even declared an unfit mother. It's a gyp."

"When you run into people from the clubs, do they speak to you?"

"They were cool to me at first, but after I did *Playboy* and was on the 'Phil Donahue Show,' some of them sided with me."

"Do you regret things?"

"The biggest mistake I made was during the trial, when I said to the kids, 'No matter what, we'll always be together,' and then I lost custody of them, and they resented it. But they're getting over that now. All my friends deserted me. People I asked to be character witnesses for me left town. Listen, I had a good time on coke for a while, up until the end, and then it turned and became bad. We stopped going to bed together, and slept at different times, and then everything fell apart.

"Jacquie Kimberly was my best friend. She and Jim and Peter and I were always together for years. Jacquie took me to Petite Marmite for lunch before the trial and said, 'The handwriting's on the wall, and I can't afford to be seen with you,' and I've never laid eyes on her again. She didn't even send me a note when I lost my kids. I can't forgive that."

There's no question in most people's minds that the girl got rooked. It takes two to tango, but the real Palm Beach closed the circle around one of their own, and the outsider got left outside with no kids, no home, and no money.

"Would you go back over the bridge to that life again?"

"The rich life? You'd have to be stupid to go down that road again."

•   •   •

Dorothy Spreckels Munn's house on North County Road is one of a pair of side-by-side mansions built in the 1920s by her late husband, Charles Munn, who was always known as Mr. Palm Beach, and his brother, Gurnee Munn, in the Spanish-Moorish style, with large rooms, wide corridors, high ceilings, and majestic stairways. Mrs. Munn, in her widowhood, has made no concessions to changing fashion in interior decoration. Entering her house is like stepping back into the thirties. A maid opened the door and directed me to a stairway, where a butler preceded me across an immense tiled hallway to a tapestry-hung library, where Mrs. Munn, two male guests, and a companion sat in what seemed to be a tableau in a time warp.

People in Palm Beach tell the story of how one night Dorothy Munn walked into a restaurant where she was well known and a favored customer. The restaurant was filled to capacity, and there was no table for her. The maître d'hotel was abject with apology, begged Mrs. Munn's forgiveness, and offered as an explanation that it was Thursday.

"Thursday?" queried Mrs. Munn.

"Cook's night out," he explained.

"Do you mean to say that all these people are cooks?" cried Mrs. Munn.

The acknowledged *grande dame* of Palm Beach, Mrs. Munn sat tall and straight-backed in a tall and straight-backed Spanish chair.

"You must have a drink," she said, looking from me to her butler.

"Perrier," I said.

"Everybody's drinking Perrier," she replied.

In recent years Mrs. Munn has absented herself from active participation in Palm Beach social life. "She doesn't go out twice a day anymore," one of her friends said to me. In Palm Beach parlance, this means she goes out either to lunch or to dinner, but never both on the same day. "You sometimes see her at people's houses, although mostly people go to her. She still loves to play cards."

"You must tell us everything about Claus von Bülow," she said to me.

"I don't think he did it," said her companion emphatically.

"Oh, I do," said one of the male guests.

"She was beautiful, Sunny," said Mrs. Munn.

Mrs. Munn is interested in writers and writing. As she has difficulty sleeping, she pays someone to read to her, some-times until as late as four in the morning. She had recently gone through the manuscript of a biography based on the life of her mother, Alma Spreckels, of the sugar family, a domi-nant figure in San Francisco society in the early decades of the century.

"How was it?" I asked.

"The dates are all there, and all the chronological order of things—she crossed the Atlantic, she did this, she did that—but there's nothing of my mother, her personality, how she was. My mother was a friend of Loie Fuller, the dancer, who was a friend of Queen Marie of Romania, and my mother and Queen Marie became friends, and . . ."

Her guests sat and listened with rapt attention.

I felt that I had finally found the Real Palm Beach.

Ava Now

"LET'S NOT TALK about Mickey, or Artie, or Frank," she said, looking up from lighting a cigarette, exhaling smoke. She was talking about Rooney, and Shaw, and Sinatra, of course, the husbands of her three brief marriages, the last of which ended in 1957. Every interview she ever gave, she said, ended up being a discussion of the same old stories, true and untrue, that had been told oh so many times. "Let's not go into the stuff you always read about me."

"O.K.," I replied.

"Is that a tape recorder?"

"Yes."

"Oh, honey, uh-uh. I'm more scared of those things than I am of the camera."

"O.K."

"Don't write," she said later when she saw me taking notes. "Let's just talk."

Ava Gardner, the ravishing love goddess of the 1950s, still has the walk, the style, and the excitement of a movie queen. Her glorious face, untouched by cosmetic surgery, is remarkably unravaged by decades of tabloid-reported riotous living. A North Carolina accent occasionally seeps through the deep, lush, MGM-trained voice, which is overlaid with a glossy international patina. She moved to London in 1968 after a long sojourn in Madrid, where she engaged in a lifestyle so flamboyant it caused her neighbors, the exiled Peróns of Argentina, to seek residence elsewhere. Time and England have brought tranquillity to her life.

It is no accident that she gravitated to this civilized nation's capital. The respect for privacy, the quieter way of life, and even the weather appeal to her. She wanders the streets of London, usually unrecognized and unintruded upon, a rootless, beautiful, fiercely American expatriate. She is a lady in retirement, but most certainly not retired. At sixty-two she is soon to make her television debut as Agrippina, the evil mother of Nero (played by Anthony Andrews), in the forthcoming NBC miniseries "A.D." She enjoyed shooting on location in Tunisia, and the possibility of a new career in a new medium looms.

Her most successful films were those in which the parts she played—like the barefoot contessa in the film of that name and Lady Brett Ashley in her friend Ernest Hemingway's *The Sun Also Rises*—meshed with the famous wild persona she created off the screen, elevating her to an almost mythic, Hollywood-star status. Her last major role was in Tennessee William's *The Night of the Iguana,* under her favorite director, John Huston. Her appearances since then have been mostly cameo roles in undistinguished films, but there is no sense of the washed-up or has-been about her. She walked away from her career but retained her stardom. Her name still evokes tremendous curiosity among the generation who adored her.

We met during a photographic session at the Launceton Place studio of Lord Snowdon in London. Although a fashionable hairdresser and a makeup man had been engaged by Lord Snowdon, Ava Gardner arrived already made up and coiffed—she had done her face and hair herself. She claimed she was nervous about the sitting, but she seemed to enjoy the experience. In a magical star gesture, a throwback to her MGM days, she signed the photo release form as if she were bestowing an autograph at a premiere.

Later we walked from the studio, in Kensington, to her home, in Knightsbridge, through back streets and mewses and across parks. She knows London like a tour guide. Stepping off a curb, I looked left instead of right, in the American manner, and nearly got nipped by a passing taxi. "You better

hold my hand," she said with a smile, and held it out to me.
We stopped to visit her veterinarian on the way; some pills
he had prescribed for her corgi were causing listlessness.
"You'll like Keith," she said to me about the veterinarian.
Waiting for Keith, who was in conference, she talked about
homeopathic cures for pets with a woman who had two gray
cats in a box. Midway through the conversation I saw the
moment of recognition in the woman's eyes when she realized
she was talking with Ava Gardner. But with true English tact
she suppressed her delight.

Ava Gardner's apartment is in a cream-colored Victorian
mansion that faces on a communal garden. "The king of
Malaysia lives in that house when he's in London," she said,
pointing out a neighboring building. For obvious reasons
there is a made-up name on the outside bell of her house. She
buzzed a signal upstairs—two shorts and a long, or two longs
and a short.

"Señora?" came the voice through the speaker.

"Si, Carmen," she replied, and we were buzzed in to the
downstairs hall. Upstairs a door opened, and the corgi barked
with a wild excitement—matched by his mistress's cries of
greeting. She calls the corgi Morgan, after her American
business manager.

Carmen, uniformed, who has been with her for years, stood
at the front door and acknowledged an affectionate introduc-
tion. The apartment is extremely handsome, with large rooms
and wide halls. Elaborately curtained windows open onto a
long, shrub-planted balcony that fronts the house. Marble-
topped consoles, gilt mirrors, lacquered cabinets. French and
Regency chairs and Chinese screens fill the rooms in actressy
splendor. The dining room is book-lined. A drink tray with
ice and glasses had been set on a table in the drawing room,
where a fire blazed invitingly. It is a very well run household.

There we were finally, settled in, strangers meeting. She
smoked constantly, selecting each cigarette from a Georgian
silver box and using a heavy cut-glass and ormolu table lighter
in the shape of a pineapple. Lighting a cigarette is a two-

handed operation, almost ritualistic, occupying her attention totally. It is another movie-star gesture in the grand tradition.

She avoids the social whirl and first nights of London life, preferring to pop in on her small coterie of friends when they are not entertaining. She attends the ballet, opera, and theater in preview performances, often with her neighbor and great friend, the English actor Charles Gray, who lives so close by that they talk to each other from their balconies. I asked about her celebrated friendships with Robert Graves, Tennessee Williams, Noel Coward, Maria Callas, and, of course, Hemingway and Huston. She smiled in recollection. "Those weren't day-to-day friendships, not through thick and thin," she said, and then added, "but they were intense on the occasions we met."

She has a habit of speaking to her dog to convey messages to you or to avoid questions she considers invasions of privacy. I told her a gossipy story a mutual friend of ours had told me involving adultery and black satin lingerie and duplicity. She clearly didn't see the need for the story to have been told, either by our mutual friend to me or by me to her, and told her dog so: "That's not a nice story." It dawned on me that Ava Gardner, who was the subject of so much gossip for so many years, never gossiped herself. Once, when the name of someone who had not behaved well with her came up, a look crossed her face that told me she had a lot she could say about that person, but she said nothing.

It is the reason she will never write a book, although offers are constant. Several unauthorized biographies have been written about her, but she scoffed at them, saying they were written from gossip columns and reviews of her pictures. Despite her strong sense of forthrightness, she disapproves of the kind of sexually graphic autobiographies that certain actresses of her generation have written, telling all, naming names.

Late at night, walking again, we went into a crowded pub. The mass of young patrons did not part for the entrance of the bareheaded, mink-jacketed star with a corgi on a leash, and I searched her face for disappointment, but found none.

"She seeps into you in a haunting kind of way," her friend Roddy McDowall said about her, and it is true. She is by turns complicated and mysterious, direct and honest, witty and melancholy. "I haven't taken an overdose of sleeping pills and called my agent," she said, quoting a much repeated line of hers from times past. "I haven't been in jail, and I don't go running to a psychiatrist every two minutes. That's something of an accomplishment, isn't it?"

Hide-and-Seek
with Diane Keaton

DIANE KEATON, the most reclu-
sive star since Garbo, does not sit in positions of relaxation.
All during our interview she seemed poised for flight, one
patent-leather-shod foot in constant motion as she goes reluc-
tantly through this chore of stardom. A pile of curls bobs on
her forehead when she speaks, and a single, purple, plastic
hoop earring jiggles from her lobe. She is prettier than she
photographs, and friendly, but wary. She pushes up, pulls
down, then pushes up again the sleeves of her blouse, dying
to be finished with the task at hand.

She lives in a glass aerie high above Central Park. Stepping
off the elevator into the foyer outside her front door, one is
immediately confronted with evidence of her unique style—
a large, track-lit artwork, which, on closer inspection, turns
out to be hundreds and hundreds of yellow plastic bananas,
piled in a corner by the actress herself. The apartment is white
on white on white, floor, ceiling, walls, kitchen tiles, furniture, even the thick diner cups and saucers—its starkness
broken by several huge floor vases of flowers and by arrangements of art objects that have caught her eye, such as a plastic
bust of Pope John Paul II that she found in a curio shop in
Toronto, a trio of reindeer that she saw at a roadside stand
while driving through Massachusetts, and a grouping of huge
papier-mâché boulders that she got in a theatrical-prop shop.
"I'm sort of a junk collector," she tells me. "What I really
need is a warehouse. I like to change things around. For a

while it's fun to look at them, and then I don't want to look at them anymore." For the moment, at least, her critically admired collages and photographs have been packed away in a back room, and she is disinclined to let me see them. There is a sense of fastidious neatness throughout—no clutter, no books or pictures littering the tabletops—and, of course, her Academy Award is nowhere in sight. Her home is like an art gallery, with changing shows.

The apartment has a 360-degree view of the city; it looks down twenty floors onto the park's sailing pond on one side, onto the copper green turrets of the majestic Dakota on another, across the West Side to the Hudson River on the third, and smack into the windows of the matching twin-tower apartment of Mary Tyler Moore on the fourth.

"Do you wave to each other?" I ask.

"Oh no. We've never met," she replies. "In fact, I've never even seen her."

Since the place is high up, safe, spacious, and very private, I am surprised when she says it is on her mind to move. She explains that the large living room, with its thirties bamboo-and-canvas furniture, and the dining area, with its huge table and chairs on casters, are pleasant but functionless rooms for her kind of life. "I never entertain," she says. She does, however, share the apartment with three large old cats, each with its own domain. She says she would like to own a loft or a building where she could have more room for work—a studio for her photography, space to edit her documentary films, and an office for her production company, where she could meet with writers to discuss projects. After nearly twenty years in New York, she tells me, she sometimes toys with the thought of returning to California to live. Then she breaks off, saying, "Listen, it's cat-hair city here. You're going to hate me when you leave."

Keaton is much more at ease talking about other people, like Mel Gibson, the hot costar of her latest movie, *Mrs. Soffel*, than about herself. "It was not difficult for me to imagine what it was like to be hopelessly in love with Mel," she says. "It was wonderful for me to play opposite him. I didn't have any idea how much emotional range he had."

Mrs. Soffel is, according to her, "a big love story," based on a true event that took place in Pittsburgh in 1901. Keaton, who plays the wife of a prison warden, gives an extraordinary and disturbing performance as a fervently religious woman who falls madly, hopelessly in love with a condemned bank robber so handsome that women wait outside the prison to send gifts in to him by the guards. Without thought of consequence, she helps the outlaw and his brother to escape and then willingly forsakes husband, children, and reputation to accompany the pair on an ill-fated, three-day race with death. The part is shocking and fascinating and a risky one for a star. Who could care about a woman who does what Mrs. Soffel does? As Diane Keaton plays the part, you may not approve, but you do understand.

She loved the role. "The idea of playing someone who had never been touched emotionally or romantically in her whole life and then gives way to an urge so strong that she cannot help herself—all the terror and excitement of it was wonderful for me." The smoldering presence of Gibson combines with Keaton's enigmatic and elusive quality to create the kind of sexual sparks that are rarely seen on the screen.

During the long and arduous shooting in Canada in twenty-degree weather, the two stars admired each other's talent but did not socialize together in their free time. "I never got to know Mel very well," says Keaton. "I wanted to keep a distance from being friendly with him. If you start hanging out together you lose the kind of tension it takes to play a part like that."

With *Reds, Shoot the Moon, The Little Drummer Girl,* and *Mrs. Soffel,* Diane Keaton has put her Annie Hall image to rest forever. Gone is every vestige of the beloved character created by Woody Allen and based on her own skittish and jittery personality. At thirty-nine, she is a major star at the peak of her talent.

"She is the dream actress that every director should have," says Gillian Armstrong, the Australian director of My Brilliant Career, who made her American directorial debut with Mrs. Soffel. "In a practical sense she is absolutely professional. There's none of that sort of star business about being late or not turning up or staying out all night, or any of those things. She is absolutely dedicated and hardworking, and she gave me the same intensity in take after take."

Working back-to-back on The Little Drummer Girl and Mrs. Soffel meant being out of the country on distant locations for nearly a year. "I don't want to do that ever again," says Keaton. "I don't want to go away and work for months and months and move every two weeks to another hotel in another country and be away from people that I love. I don't want to do that. I felt like I'd left my life for quite some time. I felt alone."

After a series of heavily dramatic roles, she longs to play comedy again, but finding the right script has not been easy. "I was spoiled by Woody," she says. At the age of twenty-three, she was cast by Allen in the stage version of Play It Again, Sam, and she later acted the same role on the screen. She also appeared with him in Sleeper, Love and Death, and the brilliant Annie Hall, for which she received an Academy Award in 1978. Her relationship with Woody Allen, both professional and romantic, remains a pivotal part of her career and life. Long apart, they have managed to maintain their friendship even through other relationships, including Allen's long liaison with Mia Farrow.

"In the comedy zone there's nobody like Woody," she continues. "I just had great roles. I would love more than anything to do a comedy again. I'd love it. But for some reason, I don't know . . ." Her voice drifts off.

So far her own attempts at developing a comedy for herself have not been successful. The most promising was called Modern Bride, a romantic comedy about a thirty-six-year-old woman who is getting married for the first time just as her parents are getting divorced. She would have coproduced and starred, but after several attempts at a script, including one by Nora Ephron and Alice Arlen and another by John Sayles, the project fell into abeyance.

Another film idea, a comedy about friendship, would star Keaton with two close friends, the actress Kathryn Grody (wife of actor Mandy Patinkin) and Carol Kane, whom she met when the three of them were in the film *Harry and Walter Go to New York.* "I'm going to stick with trying to do something with these projects, but to be honest with you," says Keaton wistfully, "I think my skills as a producer, or a person who is able to get a movie together, and get it on, and actually realize it, are . . . uh . . . it's not my . . . uh . . . gift, or, I don't think I have those capabilities in putting people together to make it happen. Now, there's a long sentence."

When talking about herself, she sometimes borders on the inarticulate, expressing self-doubt, stopping, starting, changing direction, interrupting her thoughts, advancing in disorder.

"I'm not going to quit," she says. "I'm going to continue to try to be in a movie that's funny. I'd love to do something with Woody and Mia." She jumps up from the sofa and looks out the window.

"These serious movies are hard on me. I find acting not . . . uh . . . not . . . uh . . . oh, I don't know. It's hard. It's very hard, and it brings out things in me that I don't like, which is . . . uh . . . steady, constant worry. I just worry every day. Am I O.K.? Am I all right? Look . . . I don't want to say that it's not a privilege, and it's not something I don't want to do, because I do like doing it, really, but I'm glad I'm not doing it right now."

I went to see her again in Los Angeles, where, the press agent for *Mrs. Soffel* told me, she was producing a documentary.

"What kind of documentary?"

"You'll have to let Diane tell you that. It's a private thing she's doing."

"Can't you tell me what it's about?"

"Heaven."

"Heaven?"

"Heaven."

"What about heaven?"

"You better ask her when you get out there."

She was at a hotel in Santa Monica called the Shangri-La. The nonconformist movie crowd, who have always eschewed the splendors of the Beverly Hills, Beverly Wilshire, and Bel-Air hotels in favor of the bohemian atmosphere of the Chateau Marmont, have of late picked up on the offbeat, seaside charm of Shangri-La. Built in the forties as an apartment hotel, it has been handsomely transformed into a hotel in the Art Moderne style, and it has become Keaton's favorite stopping-off place. "Diane likes the funkier kind of places," says Kathryn Grody.

When I arrived at the Shangri-La, Keaton stuck her head around a corner and called out, "Hi!" indicating the direction of her suite with a head gesture. The sleek gray living room in forties-streamline revival suited her. Her clothes have a distinctly rummage-sale/swap-meet look about them, but there is an eye for design in the layering, which is as complicated and of a piece as one of her performances. That day she was a study in black and white: a mid-calf, houndstooth-check skirt over black leggings, white push-down socks that flopped onto black patent-leather "Thriller" shoes, a black blouse pushed up at the sleeves, a black-and-white hair rag tied in a bow atop her head in a style somewhere between Carmen Miranda and Cyndi Lauper, and one hoop earring. She is often able to walk unnoticed on the street. Neither needing nor wanting to be recognized, she is assimilated into the anonymity she craves without resorting to the movie-star disguise of oversize sunglasses and fur coat. It is perhaps her bizarre manner of dressing that protects her, drawing, as it does, the gaze of passersby to her clothes rather than her face.

"Look out here," she said, gesturing again with her head. Outside, a terrace ran the length of her penthouse suite. Across Ocean Avenue were giant palm trees on the palisades. Far below was the broad Santa Monica Beach, and beyond it the Pacific Ocean. The sky was blue and cloud-filled, the scene picture-postcard beautiful.

"Great, huh?" she asked, leaning on the rail, looking out at the sea, serene, content, enjoying the moment.

It was.

"I have this longing to be here again," she said quietly. "I'd like to have a place right here in Santa Monica. I like the whole area. I like the little mall where you walk around. I can walk to a store. I can walk to a restaurant. And, of course, there's the water. I guess everybody loves Santa Monica now, though, don't they? It's the place."

After a pause, she said, "Maybe I will come back. My family's out here." Her family, with whom she is deeply involved, consists of her mother, father, two sisters, brother, and grandmother, ninety-three-year-old Grammy Hall. Her family name is Hall, but she took her mother's maiden name of Keaton because there was already a Diane Hall in Actors' Equity.

"Let me put on some water for coffee," she said, going to the bathroom for water. Her coffee machine was brand-new and unfamiliar, and she continued to talk as she tried to make it work, and then apologized for the coffee. "It's not hot enough, is it? It never really boils. Is it too strong? I don't have any cream or sugar."

"Hungry?" I asked.

"Yeah."

Not far from the Shangri-La, in the trendy Venice art colony, is the new restaurant of the moment, 72 Market Street, owned by actor-producer Tony Bill, Dudley Moore, and two partners, and backed by such celebrities as Liza Minnelli. It is the place where everyone wants to go and no one can get a table.

"Do you mind if I drop your name?" I asked before calling for a reservation.

"It won't help," she replied.

"Yes it will."

It did.

The restaurant is spacious and stunning and makes, the maître d' said, an architectural statement. We were ushered in in grand style and well seated, although Keaton makes a point of wanting no special treatment. "She disavows all the trappings of fame," says writer Lynn Grossman, one of her close friends. She would never, ever, use her name to get into a crowded restaurant in New York. "She's not waiting for heads to turn at the Russian Tea Room," says Kathryn Grody. She stands in line at the movies and has been known to decline offers by theater managers to pass her in ahead of the crowd. Sometimes she seems almost too good to be true, for a movie star. A well-known New York playwright received a letter from her, rejecting his play, that he said was the nicest letter he had ever received, so nice that he wrote her back thanking her for it, saying that her letter was better than his play. She is so shy that at 1985's Toronto film festival's Tribute to Warren Beatty, her former great love, she remained hidden in the audience and refused to be acknowledged, not even standing to wave when Beatty himself introduced her from the stage. And it is a known fact that in the newspaper ads for *Reds*, of Keaton and Beatty embracing, it was her wish that only the back of her head be shown.

"Don't you enjoy being famous?" I asked.

"I think I like to deny it. It suits me to deny it. It's more comfortable for me to deny it, but I suppose that's another one of my problems. Look, I don't think it's such a big deal, I don't think I'm that big a thing. You know, uh, I'm a movie star. I get to play the leads in movies, or I have so far, maybe not so much, you know, after, uh, whatever. . . . But I don't

feel I'm one of those prime . . . uh . . . people don't really
. . . uh . . . I don't get a lot of . . . uh . . . I mean I can
walk down the street, it's no big deal. For the most part,
people don't stop me. They kind of treat me nice. You see,
I'm not an idol or anything like that. They don't bother me.
Sure, it's great to be . . . uh . . . I'm really lucky, obviously
I'm really fortunate, and I'm grateful, but I think it's nice not
to be too well known. I hope I can continue like that."

"You're pretty well known, Diane."

"Pretty well known, but not *recognizably* well known. It's
not like being Woody Allen. 'That's Woody Allen,' they say.
Or Mary Tyler Moore. Now, *she's* famous. Or Jack Nicholson.
He's the most comfortable person being a movie star I've ever
seen. I've never seen anybody like him. I'm a big fan of his.
He's got the right attitude about it, you know, being famous.
He says, 'This is what I do, and having your picture taken,
and being recognized, it's all part of it.' "

When she travels, she takes driving trips with her friends
to places like the Grand Canyon or New Mexico, or to Mem-
phis to see Graceland, Elvis Presley's home. She loves to
drive. "She likes any odd, out-of-the-way, eccentric nook or
cranny, like the diner most people wouldn't stop at," says
Kathryn Grody, a frequent traveling companion. Lynn Grossman, who accompanied Diane to Graceland, says she enjoys
"hanging out, eating fries at roadside stands, singing songs.
She's a middle-class girl with the soul of an artist." They say
they have never seen her be rude to a fan, "even under the
most gross conditions."

In both *Shoot the Moon* and *Mrs. Soffel,* Keaton acts moth-
erhood as well as it has ever been acted, but she has no
children. Does she want them?

"Yeah, well, sure. . . . You know, I'm thirty-nine, and I
don't know how much time, I mean, there's still time. Early
on I made a career choice, and now I hope it's not too late.
Sure I do. Yes, I'd like to."

Her personal life remains her own, and intrusions are not
welcome. Recently there have been items in gossip columns

linking her romantically with a young director whom she was said to be taking home to meet her family. When I showed her the clippings, which she had not seen, she shrugged off the stories with a smile. "Oh, that Liz," she said in mock exasperation, meaning Liz Smith, in whose column one of the items had appeared.

These are areas she does not wish to share. Don't bring up Warren Beatty, I had been told in advance by one of her closest friends. She doesn't want to talk about Warren. Nevertheless, questions about their famous romance, now ended, were churning in my mind, should the moment present itself. Did Warren take her away from Woody? Does Woody hate Warren? Is it true that Woody's movie *Zelig*, with its famous people commenting on the nonentity Zelig, was meant to be a send-up of Warren's movie *Reds?* Questions like that. But where to begin?

"Have you . . . uh . . . remained friends with Warren?" I asked, feeling my way.

She changed her position, breathed in deeply, and withdrew into her privacy. For an endless moment, we waited in silence as she moved the carpaccio around on her plate. "Let me say this," she answered finally. "The experience of making *Reds* is one that I will always treasure. I have the deepest respect for Warren, both as a director and as an actor. *Reds* is a film that I am very proud of."

"And that's it on Warren?" I asked, sensing a note of termination.

"Yeah," she answered, drawing out the word.

"Let's talk about heaven," I volunteered.

"Oh, sure, heaven," she said with evident enthusiasm for the subject of her new documentary, and our awkward moment vanished.

"I've seen films depicting heaven, and there were extraordinary visual images. The whole notion of heaven frightened the hell out of me, so I thought maybe it would be interesting to put together a little documentary where you just ask everybody, as many different kinds of people as possible, what they think about heaven and how they feel about it."

She found the people around Hollywood Boulevard, and on the streets, and at various associations and churches. "I think a lot of people are afraid to think about what it's like after death. They hope for something more, but a lot of people are afraid to think about it."

"Who talks to the people and asks the questions?"

"I do."

"As Diane Keaton?"

"Oh, no, just an off-camera voice, although some of the people did call me Diane. It's a talking-heads kind of movie. We shot a lot of film. It's going to be a huge editing job."

"How much will it cost?"

"Oh, gosh, a lot."

"Who's paying for it?"

"One of the cable stations."

"Would you call that one of the perks of fame?"

"Yeah," she answered. "That's the good part, being able to do things like this little documentary, and publishing my books on photography."

It was late. Back at the Shangri-La we said good-bye. She was going that evening to the new Los Angeles Museum of Contemporary Art for the viewing of a laser work donated by her friend Doug Wheeler. Watching her retreat into the lobby, I was struck by her walk and by her extraordinary style, which no one else could ever quite bring off the way she does. I liked her. I missed her already.

The next day, before returning to New York, I caught up with family at the hotel for lunch. When Beverly Hills people say "the hotel," they mean only the Beverly Hills Hotel. It is the hub of activity, where you buy the *New York Times*, get your shoes shined, have breakfast, lunch, or dinner, and run into a wide assortment of people. At the entrance to the Polo

Lounge, talking to Pasquale, the maître d', I saw the back of a woman wearing a black-and-white houndstooth-check skirt over black leggings, white push-down socks falling onto Thriller shoes, and a black-and-white hair rag tied in a style somewhere between Carmen Miranda and Cyndi Lauper. It was Diane Keaton, who, her friends had assured me, never, ever went to places like the Beverly Hills Hotel. We said hello again.

Later, during lunch, heads turned in the Polo Lounge as Warren Beatty entered the room. He has the kind of star presence that even the most sophisticated people do not take in their stride.

"Hi," he said to me in passing. "I hear you had an interesting day yesterday." He continued on through the Polo Lounge to the glass door that opens out to the terrace. At the farthest end of the patio, he sat down at the table where Diane Keaton was waiting. They have, it appeared, remained friends.

Kim Sargent, Palm Beach Daily News

"She's Mollie Netcher Bragno Bostwick Wilmot [*left*]. She lives next to Rose Kennedy, and last year a tanker ran aground on her seawall and practically landed in her living room....That elderly lady, Mary Sanford [*right*], Laddie Sanford's widow—you know, the polo player. They call her the Queen of Palm Beach. Don't say I called her elderly."

(*above left*) "C.Z. Guest, Mrs. Winston Guest, the famous gardener. She's become rather independent down here." (*above right*) "Her daughter, Cornelia Guest, who's always in the papers."

(*above left*) Gregg Dodge, who went through $13.5 million. "Mary Sanford and I used to run this town socially. Nobody gave a party without checking with us first." (*above right*) Sue Whitmore, who is never not referred to as the Listerine heiress, spends her time in Palm Beach, Greenwich, and Saratoga, and in the summer lives on a yacht in Newport. Is her yacht big? "Big to some, small to others."

Celia Lipton Farris, whose late husband invented the milk carton. "Nowadays anyone with money can get in the Shiny Sheet. I was raised in England, so I learned to say please and thank you two days after I was born."

Jim Kimberly, Roxanne Pulitzer, and Jacquie Kimberly. Roxanne fell from grace after her divorce from Peter Pulitzer in 1982. "All my friends deserted me. Jacquie Kimberly was my best friend. She took me to Petite Marmite for lunch before the trial and said, 'The handwriting's on the wall, and I can't afford to be seen with you.' "

Ava Gardner in London. Time and England have brought tranquillity to her life.

Diane Keaton. "I find acting not...uh...not...uh...ooh, I don't know. It's hard. It's very hard, and it brings out things in me that I don't like which is...uh...steady, constant worry. I just worry every day. Am I O.K.? Am I all right?"

Elizabeth Taylor prepares for her *Vanity Fair* cover session with makeup man Jacques Clemente, hairdresser Alexandre de Paris, and Dominick Dunne.

''I can't remember when I wasn't famous.''

By Alex Gotfryd

Gloria Vanderbilt, the poor little rich girl of the thirties, is very much in control of her life in the eighties.

Lunch at Sunny von Bülow's New York apartment during Claus von Bülow's trial for her attempted murder. Left to right are Helmut Newton, Carlos Merlo, Dominick Dunne, von Bülow, Christian Gudefin, Cosima von Bülow, and Andrea Reynolds.

Helmut Newton/SYGMA

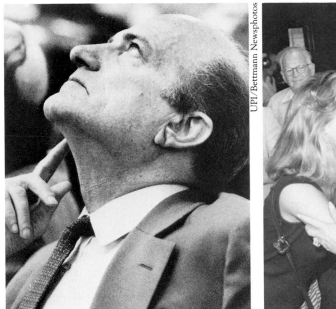

(*above left*) Claus von Bülow during his second trial. Says a close friend, "Claus is trompe l'oeil." (*above right*) Claus von Bülow after his acquittal, as his daughter by his wife, Sunny, kisses his mistress, Mrs. Reynolds. "No new woman in my life could have survived a lack of affinity with Cosima."

Mrs. Reynolds flashes a victory sign after the jury reached a verdict of not guilty. Says her husband, Sheldon Reynolds, "If Claus has to marry Andrea, he will wish he'd been convicted."

The Red Queen

⟨⟨✦⟩⟩

IN 1972, IN Cortina d'Am-
pezzo, a mountain resort in the Italian Dolomites, Elizabeth
Taylor, Henry Fonda, and Helmut Berger starred in a film I
produced called *Ash Wednesday*. Elizabeth was then in the
waning period of the first of her two marriages to Richard
Burton. Being with the Burtons, as they were always called,
was like being in a state of almost surreal celebrity. Late late
one night, during an all-stops-out conversation, Elizabeth said
to me, "You know, I can't remember when I wasn't famous."
It was a statement made without the slightest braggadocio,
simply as a fact of her celebrated life. Except for that other
Elizabeth, the queen of England, who else, then or now,
could make it?

In September of this year I went to the London home of
Elizabeth's film-producer friend Norma Heyman, where Elizabeth was staying, to take her to the photo session for this
article. The photographer Helmut Newton was there, along
with the dozen or so necessary people who arrange her hair
and make up her face and provide her clothes and carry her
jewels. We waited four hours for her to get ready, drinking
pots of coffee, passing the Sunday papers back and forth across
the kitchen table. "Elizabeth is chronically late," Richard
Burton once said about her. Her lateness is as much a part of
her as her violet eyes. Bulletins from above were sent down
from time to time. She had slept on her left side, and her left
eye was puffed up. Were there cucumbers in the house? Were
there tea bags? She had not liked all the Yves Saint Laurent

dresses sent over from Paris. She had called in the Emanuels. More than once Helmut Newton wondered if the already problematic light would last.

Finally, of course, she appeared, descending the stairway in great good humor, unperturbed by the chaos she causes, and all, as always, was instantly forgiven in the wake of her never diminishing splendor. Even if you know Elizabeth Taylor, it is not uncustomary to gasp a little when you see her. She is a sight that never ceases to fascinate. Now, in the forty-third year of her stardom, she is voluptuous and ravishing again. The recent image of obesity and alcoholism and Percodan addiction is behind her. Except for her recurring back problems, she radiates good health and a maturing beauty. "Sheran sends her love," she said to me about her childhood friend Sheran Cazalet Hornby, at whose country house she had spent the weekend. Unhurried, she examined herself in a hall mirror, the left side of her face, the right side of her face, moistened her lips, evened her lipstick with the little finger of her left hand, and adjusted a strand of her frosted black hair.

"There are lots of *paparazzi* in front of the house," I said to alert her.

"So what else is new?" she answered.

"You look great."

"Thank you, love."

Outside, the sky was suddenly bright for the first time that day.

"You see, the sun is better now," she said to Helmut Newton, as if she had done him a favor by being late.

"You're torturing me," he replied.

"No, I'm toying with you," she said.

Trained like royalty to understand and undertake the obligations of her calling, she moved forward to the reporters and news photographers waiting for her in front of the house. She stopped, smiled, waved, posed, and spoke to the ones she recognized.

"How is Rock Hudson?" asked an English reporter.

She shrugged and blinked slowly, as if her eyelids were suddenly weighty.

"Have you visited him?"

"Yes."

"Will he get better?" persisted the reporter.

"No," she replied. With her security man, her secretary, and her chauffeur in attendance, she moved on into her Rolls-Royce and raced across London for the picture session.

If she understands the duties of a star, she also expects the perks of a star, as she demonstrated at the end of the session.

"I want the red dress," she said to the woman who had arranged the sitting. As she spoke she adjusted her makeup in the mirror, moving her little finger back and forth over her lipstick.

"The Emanuel?"

"No," she said, "I already have that."

"The Yves Saint Laurent?"

"Yes."

"I don't really have the authority," the magazine's representative said.

"Ask," she said with the perfect certainty that the dress would be hers. (It was.)

Her permanent home these days is Los Angeles, where she grew up as a child star at MGM and where she returned in 1982 to reestablish her roots. Her house, which is hidden from view, set behind gates equipped with closed-circuit television to screen callers, once belonged to Nancy Sinatra, Sr. Taylor bought it for $2 million after separating from her sixth husband, United States Senator John Warner. From her terrace one looks out over the hills of Bel Air onto Los Angeles below. The house is both sprawling and simple, elegant and comfortable. A living room opens into a game room, which opens into a dining room. The first floor is monochromatically decorated in off-white; all the color comes from her art collection and a profusion of enormous orchid plants in full purple bloom.

On a lacquered table in the game room are silver-framed photographs of her: being greeted by the queen of England, talking with President Gerald Ford, laughing with Marshal Tito, being welcomed at the Iranian Embassy in Washington by her onetime suitor Ambassador Ardeshir Zahedi, posing festively at Ascot with Richard Burton and Noel Coward in gray top hats. There is an inscribed photograph from Princess Grace and Prince Rainier of Monaco, another from David Niven. Her two Oscars, for *Butterfield 8* and *Who's Afraid of Virginia Woolf?* are prominently displayed in the center of bookshelves crammed with other, lesser awards.

While I waited for her in the living room, Liz Thorburn, who runs her house, brought tea and placed a fresh pack of Salems, opened, with several cigarettes pushed forward for easy access, in front of the place on the sofa where Elizabeth would sit. Next to it she placed a lighter. A Cordon Bleu chef, the Scottish Miss Thorburn, young and attractive, formerly worked at Kensington Palace for Princess Margaret. "I've gone from a princess to a queen," she observed with a twinkle in her eye. In contrast to the glamorous chaos of the old life-style I associated with Elizabeth Taylor—trunks being packed and unpacked constantly—this was the well-run, very organized household of a woman settled in her own surroundings with her own things.

No one who knows Elizabeth Taylor ever calls her Liz. Used to homage, she did not remember to thank me, when she arrived, for a $100 bouquet of flowers in her favorite color, lavender, which I had sent her, and which was nowhere in sight. She was dressed in pink silk lounging pajamas and flat-heeled shoes instead of the spikes she habitually wears. It is always surprising to realize how small this majestic woman actually is. Her only jewelry was the thirty-three-carat Krupp diamond that Richard Burton gave her, which she wears day and night, dressed up or dressed down. Her face was deeply tanned, but her beautiful skin seemed to bear no ill effects from the California sun. Her figure nearly retained the slimness she had achieved last year, when she lost forty-five pounds in two months on a diet program of her own devising. "I read in the paper that someone had a fat picture of me on her refrigerator door to keep her from eating, and I said to myself, well, if it helps her, it ought to help me. You should see the awful picture I have of myself on the icebox door. I don't crave booze at all," she added, "but I do crave sweet things."

Her reverence for Richard Burton, who died last year, is absolute, and private, and she was emphatic in stating that she did not wish to share her thoughts and feelings about him. Her stare is unflinching when she makes such a point. In an interview, even a friendly one, she is on her guard. "I've been burned so many times," she warned me. She said she had never read Kitty Kelley's book *Elizabeth Taylor: The Last Star.* "I've been told I should sue, but it would mean reading the book, and I just can't stomach it." If there were long moments of silence, she did nothing to fill them in. At other times, on certain subjects, she said, "This is off the record," or motioned for the tape recorder to be turned off, with the expertise of someone who had been through the procedure a thousand times before. Several times she pulled out a handbag from behind some pillows and brushed on pink lipstick as a way of changing the subject. When I asked her about her short-term, highly publicized engagement last year to Frank Sinatra's crony Dennis Stein, she said into her mirror, "Let's just say I almost made a mistake," and then added, "but I didn't."

Settled among the soft cushions of her deep sofa, she lit a cigarette. "My only vice," she explained, inhaling deeply. On the wall behind her were a Modigliani, a Renoir, a Van Gogh, a Rouault, a Degas, and a Monet. Elsewhere in the room Utrillos, Vlamincks, and other treasures hung. Her late father, Francis Taylor, ran an art gallery in London and Beverly Hills when Elizabeth was a child, and her knowledge of art was formed early. There are other evidences of wealth. She owns two racehorses, and the racing colors she chose, cerise and chartreuse, are the colors she wore in *National Velvet*. In the driveway outside was her new car, an Aston Martin Lagonda, for which she had paid $153,000, on the spot, one day when she went shopping for a Rolls. "It's all money I've earned," she said. "I've never asked for alimony in my life."

Chief among her accomplishments over the last several years was her seven-week stay at the Betty Ford Center near Palm Springs. Her admiration for Betty Ford is boundless. "My God, what she's done for women alcoholics is just phenomenal! She's lifted the stigma." She went to the center through family intervention. She was at Saint John's Hospital in Santa Monica when her brother and his wife, her sons, and one of her daughters arrived to tell her that she could go to the Betty Ford Center by choice or she would eventually end up killing herself. She admits to being riddled with guilt and shame, but the decision to go was her own.

Like most people who have conquered an addiction, she talked openly and freely about it, without embarrassment, aware that the example she had set was a help to other people.

"I'd been taking sleeping pills every night for thirty-five years. I was hooked on Percodan. I had reached a point where I would take one or two Percodan mixed with booze before I could go out in the evening and face people. I think you know how horribly shy I really am. I thought it would help me, because that combination would make me kind of talkative. I felt I was being charming. I was probably boring as hell, but it gave me false courage.

"During the course of an evening, like every four hours, I'd take another two Percodan. And, of course, I had a hollow leg. I could drink anybody under the table and never get drunk. My capacity to consume was terrifying. I didn't even realize that I was an alcoholic until I'd been at the center for a couple of weeks. Just because I wouldn't get drunk doesn't mean it wasn't poison for me."

"How soon after you went to the Betty Ford Center did the press pick up that you were there?" I asked.

"I'd been there over a week, but I have an uncanny sense about the press. I had a feeling in my gut that it was going to leak out, so I talked to Betty Ford about it, and she agreed that I should announce it and get it in print, because otherwise the press would make up a story about me being in a straitjacket, or carried down, or God knows what. I was right. They were onto it, but I beat them by a few hours."

"What was your first encounter with the other people there like? You must have caused a sensation."

"They'd never had a celebrity before. They told me later, the counselors, they didn't know what to do with me, whether they should treat me like an ordinary patient or whether they should give me some sort of special isolated treatment. They decided to lump me in with everyone else, which of course was the only way to do it, and it's the way they treat celebrities now. It doesn't matter who you are. We get all kinds down there: street junkies, preachers, priests, doctors, psychiatrists, and society ladies—you name it."

"Was it hard for you to talk in front of those people?"

"In the beginning, yes. I felt like I was giving interviews. I talked about my childhood and my past in a very couched way, giving the version I would give to the press and keeping the true version to myself. And then I broke all those barriers down and told the truth. Like an onion, I was peeled down to the absolute core."

"Did you have a roommate?" I asked.

"Yes," she replied, then thought about it for a moment and added with a smile, "It was the first time in my life I'd ever shared a room with a woman."

Relaxed now, she sank deeper into the cushions and lit another cigarette. Her Pekingese, complete with lavender bow, passed through the room. Her Burmese cat walked across the top of the sofa, down her arm, and settled comfortably in her lap. "Don't you love the way cats come in and insinuate

themselves on you?" she said. "Who do you think you are?"
she said to the cat. For a while we sat without talking.

"There's a nice feeling in this house," I said.

"I love this house," she replied.

"What's that room up there?" I asked, pointing across the
patio to a second-story aerie surrounded by treetops.

"That's my bedroom, and no one gets in there without an
engraved invitation."

"Hmmm."

"I suppose you want to see it?"

"Sure."

"I'll show it to you, but don't write about it."

"Elizabeth," I said to her, "this is really the first extended
period in your life when you are, uh, uh . . ."

"Single?" she asked, finishing the sentence for me.

"Yes."

"It is. I think maybe finally I'm growing up, and about time.
Being alone doesn't frighten me. And it's not like I'm alone."
Elsewhere in the house the sounds of visiting grandchildren
could be heard, and she made a movement of her head in that
direction and said with a smile, "Because I'm not."

Her attention shifted back to the cat staring up at her, and
she continued talking in measured sentences as she returned
the stare. "I'm dating several men, but I'm in no rush to get
married. I've broken two engagements. I'm being very cau-
tious. I'm sure I will remarry once more, but"—holding up
her index finger and shaking it—"*only* once more, and, boy,
it's going to be right. I'm taking no chances."

She has had seven marriages and six husbands, four of
whom are dead: hotel heir Nicky Hilton, actor Michael Wilding, showman Mike Todd, and superstar Richard Burton. Her
other husbands were singer Eddie Fisher and Senator John
Warner of Virginia. She has four children and five grandchildren. By Michael Wilding she had two sons: Michael, an
actor, who is married to Brooke Palance (daughter of Jack),
with two children by his previous marriage; and Christopher,
an artist, married to Aileen Getty, the daughter of Paul

Getty, Jr., by whom he has two children. Her daughter Liza, a sculptress, married to Hap Tivey, was born shortly before her father, Mike Todd, died in a plane crash. Her other daughter, German-born Maria, was adopted by Elizabeth and Richard Burton; she is married to agent Steve Carson and has one daughter.

An extremely handsome young child entered the room and interrupted our conversation.

"Elizabeth, can I go . . ."

"I'm busy now, love," she replied.

"But, Elizabeth," he insisted, "I want to . . ."

She gave him her full attention. "Can't you see I'm talking to Mr. Dunne? Say hello to Mr. Dunne. This is Balthazar Getty," she said to me.

Balthazar strode purposefully across the room and held out his hand. "How do you do?" he said in a manner to make a parent proud.

"Hello, Balthazar," I replied.

"Now, outside, until I finish," she said, smiling. "Stay by the pool, where I can see you."

"O.K., Elizabeth," said the child, opening and then pulling together the sliding doors to the patio. Balthazar, she explained, is the nephew of her daughter-in-law Aileen Getty Wilding. He is the son of Aileen's brother Paul Getty III, who gained international fame when his ear was cut off by kidnappers in Italy, and who subsequently became physically incapacitated after he suffered a stroke. Aileen and Christopher and their two babies were staying with Elizabeth until their new house in Bel Air was ready.

For a moment it was almost possible to believe her claim that she is semiretired from the film business, devoting herself to family life, horse racing, and good works. But anyone who knows anything about the film business knows that semiretired means simply until the next good script comes along.

Elizabeth Taylor is the national chairman of AFAR, the American Foundation for AIDS Research. On October 2,

1985, Rock Hudson, her great friend and costar in *Giant*, died of AIDS. Two weeks earlier, on September 19, Elizabeth, dressed in black lace and emeralds, entered the main ballroom of the Bonaventure Hotel in downtown Los Angeles, and three thousand of her peers rose and cheered her with a wild ovation. By lending her name and considerable support to APLA, AIDS Project Los Angeles, for the benefit entitled "Commitment to Life," she had helped raise over a million dollars in a single evening, and the huge turnout of stars that night attracted international publicity for the plight of AIDS victims.

Amid the pandemonium, she remained socially graceful, finding the right thing to say to each person she greeted, from Whoopi Goldberg to Cyndi Lauper to Burt Reynolds to Shirley MacLaine to Gregory Peck, talking intimately and laughing as if a hundred flashbulbs were not exploding in her face and security men were not holding back the crush of people who wanted to get nearer to her. "I don't want to talk to her, I just want to *look* at her!" one beautifully dressed woman pleaded with a guard.

"I'm stunned," said a young, female studio executive sitting next to me at Elizabeth's table. "I've never seen anything like this. I've been with Barbra and Jane in public, but it's nothing like this."

After four decades of making headlines with her marriages, her divorces, her tragedies, and her near-fatal illnesses, she has passed from superstardom into legend. "That comes with aging," she told me modestly. The public has seen her at the top, in the middle, and, supposedly, washed up. But Elizabeth Taylor will never be washed up. She is Ol' Man River. She just keeps on rollin' along.

Gloria's Euphoria

AT THE WINDOW table in Mortimer's on New York's Upper East Side, Jerry Zipkin, Nancy Reagan's close friend, was celebrating his seventieth birthday with a group of social figures that included Nan Kempner, Chessy Rayner, Mica and Ahmet Ertegun, and Carolina and Reinaldo Herrera, all of whom were passing elaborately wrapped gifts to him. Mica Ertegun's present, which Zipkin opened and held up, was a nineteenth-century painting of a boar, with the name Zip on a small brass plate attached to the frame, and the joke was greeted with hoots and screams from the assembled company.

At a nearby table, faced away from the merriment, sat Gloria Vanderbilt, alone, waiting for her luncheon companion. And at the bar, all the people waiting for tables were staring at her, not at the riotous party behind her.

"She looks wonderful," said a lady in a feathered hat.

"Marvelous," her friend replied.

They spoke with that proprietary tone New Yorkers reserve for a cherished celebrity—a survivor as well, in this case, against all odds of being one—who continues to cast a magic spell.

"No one told me you were here!" she cried, greeting me at the door of her red library. "Have you been waiting long?" She was contrite. She always rises before six, and at that hour, shortly after nine, she had been about the business of her life for several hours.

Gloria Laura **Morgan** Vanderbilt di Cicco Stokowski

Lumet Cooper is, like the queen of England and Elizabeth
Taylor, a lifetime celebrity, famous from childhood. She was
wearing brown cashmere, and she settled elegantly into the
corner of a chintz sofa. The great-great-granddaughter of
Commodore Cornelius Vanderbilt, who founded the family
railroad and shipping fortune, lives in a penthouse on Gracie
Square with her two teenage sons by her last husband, writer
Wyatt Cooper, who died in 1978. Outside, beyond the terrace, tugboats lumbered by under the Triborough Bridge on
the sun-dappled East River—that magical view you see so
often in movies about rich people in Manhattan.

She speaks in a breathless, whispery, society-girl voice, and
there is a trace of a stammer, under control and attractive.
Her much photographed flour-white face, so prominent at
theatrical and social parties in New York, was scrubbed and
clear. Her hair, no longer black and severe, is now chestnut-
colored, and it moved freely as she talked and gestured. She
looked healthy and fresh and much younger than her well-
documented age of sixty-one.

That evening a gossip column had announced that she
might be on the verge of marrying again, and she giggled
luxuriously over the item, her dimples deepening, her eyes
sparkling, at the same time dismissing and enjoying it. She
was, even in the morning, decidedly glamorous. She held a
gold cigarette case with a sapphire clasp that she had bought
at auction. Inside, engraved, were the words "To Gertie from
Noel" and the notes to the opening phrase of "Some Day I'll
Find You."

"Isn't it divine?" she asked. She had bought it specially for
her great friend Bill Blass, the dress designer, and had intended to leave it to him in her will, but Blass, a constant
smoker, had recently lost his own cigarette case, which had
been left to him by the late Billy Baldwin, the interior designer, so she had decided to give it to him when they met
for lunch later that day, rather than leave it to him after she
was dead.

Behind her on a red lacquered wall was a photograph of a painting of Vanderbilt ancestors, the original of which hangs at Biltmore, the massive French chateau in Asheville, North Carolina, built by her great-uncle George Vanderbilt. She said she had spotted the painting in the background of a scene in the film *Being There*, which was shot in that house, and had had it reproduced. Beneath the photograph was an etching depicting all the great Vanderbilt mansions, both town and country, erected in the early years of the century, when the Vanderbilt family was busily establishing itself as the grandest in the land.

Her large apartment on two floors has the feeling of a country house in the city. Her library and bedrooms are memorabilia-filled with heirlooms, oil portraits, and family photographs in silver frames everywhere. There is a sense of roots and permanence and of ancestors having lived in these rooms before her, but it is a performance created by Vanderbilt herself. The poor little rich girl of the thirties, who was the central figure in the most sensational child custody case in the history of the United States, never had a room of her own until she was fifteen years old. Left fatherless before she was two, on the death of the alcoholic Reginald Vanderbilt, she was shunted from hotel to hotel, from rented house to rented house, from continent to continent, by her beautiful, thoughtless, pleasure-bent, widowed young mother, Gloria Morgan Vanderbilt. When, finally, she secured a degree of permanence of location, in her aunt Gertrude Vanderbilt Whitney's vast country house, Wheatley Hills, in Old Westbury, Long Island, her assigned room, next to her aunt's, was the former room of her late uncle, the sportsman Harry Payne Whitney, which had been left intact since his death. Nothing was changed to accommodate a girl of ten, and for five years she lived with her uncle's horse prints and brown carpets, his curtains and chairs.

The dining room of Gloria Vanderbilt's apartment is dominated by a full-length portrait of her mother, painted in Paris when she was the child bride of the already dying Reginald Vanderbilt. Another painting of her mother occupies a wall of the guest room. There are photographs of her mother taken by Dorothy Wilding, the society photographer of an earlier time, and a drawing by Cecil Beaton of her mother with her equally beautiful twin sister, Thelma, Lady Furness, once the mistress of the Prince of Wales. There is, throughout the apartment, a sense of *hommage* to the woman the courts found unfit to be her mother.

She said, confidentially, about women like her mother, "You know, the kind of social strata they were in—they really in a sense were not meant to be mothers, because their instincts were not in that direction." She quotes her late husband Wyatt Cooper on her mother, when he first met her, in the final years of her life, living quietly with her twin sister in a small bungalow in Beverly Hills crammed with furniture that had once graced larger rooms: "This woman does not understand one thing that ever happened to her."

Five years ago Barbara Goldsmith wrote a highly successful book based on the *Matter of Vanderbilt,* as the custody case was legally called, entitled *Little Gloria . . . Happy at Last.* Alden Whitman, writing in the *Philadelphia Inquirer,* called it "a Proustian picture of the American upper class and the international society of which it was a part." It was a Book-of-the-Month Club main selection and for four months remained on the *New York Times* best-seller list. It was a well-known fact in New York at the time that the book greatly distressed Vanderbilt. She had refused to be interviewed by Goldsmith. "She called me, which fascinated me, and said, 'I'm ready to interview you.' I said, 'From one professional writer to another, why should I give you material? Someday I'm going to write my own book.' " She claims never to have read Goldsmith's book, saying, "I have rarely read anything about myself." She implored her friends not to read it, declined an invitation to one of hostess Alice Mason's dinners when she found out Goldsmith would be present, and even stopped speaking to one of her friends, Maureen

Stapleton, for playing the role of Dodo, her beloved nanny, in the four-hour, television miniseries based on Gold-smith's book. The story, Vanderbilt felt, was hers to tell, and the time would come when she would be ready to tell it.

Now, five years later, she had told it, in a searing personal memoir entitled *Once Upon a Time*, subtitled, "A True Story." It is the account of the celebrated, lonely child who figured at the center of the custody trial rather than the story of the trial itself. In it she records the events of her extraordinary childhood, as she remembers them, in the language of the age she was at the time of the events—a series of long-suppressed memories finally come to life. "This is the way I have chosen to tell it," she said, "because this is the way I experienced it." It is an interesting twist that the book has been brought out by the same publishing house, Knopf, that issued Goldsmith's book, and that the same editor, Bob Gott-lieb, has worked on both and managed to retain the good graces of both authors.

Even the genesis of writing the book has elements of the phantasmal quality of Vanderbilt's life. A discarded baby picture of Gloria Vanderbilt and a cousin, Emily Vanderbilt, taken in Central Park nearly sixty years ago, was saved by the maid of a relative and sent to Vanderbilt. And that picture inspired her book.

"Fate is so extraordinary," she said. "I looked at that picture of the baby in the carriage and I thought, 'I know this person. Me. I'm going to sit down and write about her.' And I did. I started writing just before the New Year, just after Christmas, and I couldn't stop writing. It was like being ob-sessed with it. And I wrote, and I wrote, and I wrote, and I finished it by April." Some days she wrote without stop for eight hours.

Throughout the book there is the sense of longing of the child for her mother. "Sometimes our hands touched," writes Vanderbilt. "But then she would go away, down the long corridors of hotels, down staircases, along avenues in her pale furs, snow-sprinkled, disappearing into the velvet caverns of waiting cars and borne away, away, away, away. . . . Would I ever see her again?"

Vanderbilt's Grandmother Morgan, her mother's mother, a curious, strong-willed woman who disapproved of her daughter's flagrant life-style, and Vanderbilt's nanny, Dodo, were the people most important to her in her early life. "No father anywhere reachable, and Mother who was always coming in and then going out—mostly going out," she writes. When her father died in Newport before her second birthday, her mother, who was only nineteen years old, was at the theater in New York City. That night the little girl was taken to the Breakers, her paternal grandmother Alice Gwynne Vanderbilt's Newport mansion.

Early on in life the susceptible child was manipulated to be frightened of her mother, principally by her nanny and her maternal grandmother, Laura Morgan, who feared that the young widow, who was in love with Prince Friedel Hohen-lohe, nephew of Queen Marie of Romania, would take the child to live in Germany. The grandmother persuaded the immensely rich and powerful sculptress Gertrude Vanderbilt Whitney, sister of Reginald and founder of the Whitney Museum of American Art, to go to court and fight with her sister-in-law over Gloria's custody. "You must show your Aunt Gertrude how much you love her," Vanderbilt quotes her grandmother as telling her. "You must hug her more and kiss her a lot."

She described arriving at the courthouse, at the age of ten, in the backseat of her aunt's gray Rolls-Royce limousine as hundreds of spectators peered in the windows and jostled the car, and then her passage up the steps as photographers took her picture and a crowd surged around her.

"Was there any thrill to that?"

"What a question! Are you mad? It was terrifying," she answered. "They were screaming, 'You treat your ma good, Little Gloria! Stick to your ma! You be nice to your ma!' "

On one occasion during the trial, when the judge allowed her mother to visit her at her aunt's house in Old Westbury, she locked herself in her room and hid the key in the bottom of a powder box so as not to have to see her. She believed mistakenly that if she were put in the custody of her Aunt Gertrude, she would have Dodo with her forever, and Dodo was the only person in the world with whom she did not feel she was an impostor. The irony of the case is that in awarding the custody of Little Gloria to her aunt instead of her mother the judge imposed as a condition of the verdict that the nanny be discharged. Gloria was not allowed to maintain any contact with her. To further the isolation caused by the verdict, Vanderbilt writes, her favorite Whitney cousin, Gerta Henry, who also lived on the estate in Old Westbury, was told by her father that she could no longer play with or be friends with Gloria, because Gloria was a bad influence, who would grow up to be exactly like her mother.

"All those people took this child and made mashed potatoes out of her, and when it was all over, everyone was back on square one," observed Vanderbilt a half-century later about the proceedings. Her mother was allowed to see her on weekends and for one month during the summer, but their meetings were strained, and most of their time together they spent going to movies. The rest of the time Vanderbilt lived in Old Westbury at her aunt's house, but once the trial was over, contact with Gertrude Whitney was minimal. "There was the time we looked at a magazine together," she remembered. "Oh, I think she loved me, but I think the tragedy of her was that she couldn't express her love."

Expressions of love were equally difficult between her and her mother in the years following the trial. In her book she writes about a July visit to her mother in Los Angeles during her early teenage years. At one point they are in the backseat of a limousine, driving up the coast of California to spend a weekend at San Simeon, the castle of William Randolph Hearst and Marion Davies. "Long before we reached Santa

Barbara," Vanderbilt writes, "my mother ran out of conversation, and when she ran out of conversation, I ran out of conversation too."

Looking out the windows to the East River, Vanderbilt explained that they went through their lives without ever once discussing the trial together, although it was the thing that had changed them all. Then she corrected herself. "Thelma did say one thing to me, actually, now that I come to think of it." Thelma, which she pronounces Telma, was her mother's twin. "She said, 'Probably Mrs. Whitney believed all those things Mama said about your mother.' Thank God my mother had Thelma, because they really were like a mirror image of each other, and not only that, but so supportive of each other. It was as if my mother and Thelma were married. When you think of it, imagine, from birth, being in a room with someone who looks exactly like you and is just there as an extension of yourself. I almost never saw my mother really alone. Thelma was always there, and I realized later that my mother was as frightened of me as I was of her. Did I tell you how Thelma died? She dropped dead on Seventy-third and Lexington on her way to see the doctor. In her bag was this miniature teddy bear that the Prince of Wales had given her, years and years before, when she came to be with my mother at the custody trial, and it was worn down to the nub."

She has, in adulthood, made her peace with her Vanderbilt and Whitney relations, from whom she felt so alienated while she was growing up. The word *impostor* keeps coming into her conversation; she felt as a child that she was in their midst under false pretenses and would be found out and banished. "I couldn't wait to grow up," she said. The past Thanksgiving, she and her sons spent the day with eighty Whitney relations in Westbury.

"The estate is all chopped up now," she said. "It's amazing what happened to it. My cousin Pam lives in Aunt Gertrude's studio now. The house where I lived, my aunt's house, is where Flora Miller lives, who is Pam's mother. And Sonny

Whitney's house and the indoor pool and the stables are a country club now. Sonny sold the estate right from under them, and they don't speak now because of that. I mean, the golf club comes right up to my cousin Flora's front lawn. From her bedroom, which was my aunt's room, she looks out and there are people in Bermuda shorts walking around."

Vanderbilt shook her head and twisted one of the three signet rings she was wearing on her fingers. "You know," she said, remembering back to the old days in Westbury, "it seemed as if it would last forever. It seemed to just happen. Effortlessly. You never saw people with vacuums or anything, and flowers would be changed overnight by unseen hands. It was just . . . perfect."

About the Vanderbilt side of the family, she said, "I'm very friendly now with all of them. In fact, every summer we go to Newport and stay at the Breakers. I hadn't been back to the Breakers since I was a child, and of course now it's a museum, with hordes of people going through. My cousin Sylvie, Countess Szapary, the daughter of my Aunt Gladys, who was my father's other sister, lives on the top floor, and I always stay in what was my father's room. It's sort of fascinating. Everything is exactly the way it was, except the tubs, those incredible bathtubs. Nothing comes out of the tap for hot salt water piped in from the sea anymore."

Once Upon a Time ends when Vanderbilt is seventeen, racing down the beach away from a Fourth of July party in Malibu, six months before the first of her four marriages to such wildly different types as actors' agent Pat di Cicco, conductor Leopold Stokowski, film director Sidney Lumet, and writer Wyatt Cooper. She was reluctant to talk about her first three marriages or her unsuccessful reunion with her nanny, Dodo, whom she hired as a nurse for the two sons of her second marriage, to Stokowski, for these are things she will be dealing with in the remaining five, or possibly six, volumes of her memoirs. The second volume, almost finished, takes her from age seventeen to twenty-one, and the third from twenty-one to twenty-nine. "I intend to live a very long life.

My Grandmother Vanderbilt lived to ninety-five, and my Grandmother Morgan to a hundred and five. Of course, she lied about her age, but we knew. People say to me that I have total recall, but everything is a relative thing. I'm also a natural-born writer. It's how you perceive it, how you invent it, how you choose to tell it."

On several occasions the late Truman Capote wrote about her. In *Breakfast at Tiffany's,* her stutter, "genuine but still a bit laid on," was supposedly the inspiration for the model Mag Wildwood, Holly Golightly's best friend. In "La Côte Basque, 1965," the most celebrated chapter of Capote's never completed novel, *Answered Prayers,* published in *Esquire* in 1975, Vanderbilt appeared as herself, together with her chum Carol Marcus Saroyan Saroyan Matthau. In the story, Vanderbilt fails to recognize her first husband, Pat di Cicco, when he stops by her table to chat.

Her close friendships with women, especially Carol Matthau and Oona Chaplin, tend to be lasting. At one time all three married much older men. Carol Matthau married writer William Saroyan twice. Oona Chaplin, daughter of playwright Eugene O'Neill, married Charlie Chaplin. And Vanderbilt wed Leopold Stokowski, who was forty years her senior. For the last few years the two women closest to her have been New York socialites Judy Peabody and Isabel Eberstadt. Like Vanderbilt, they are artistically inclined. Judy Peabody is chairman of the board of directors of the Dance Theatre of Harlem, and Isabel Eberstadt is a novelist. "I really trust women," said Vanderbilt. "And I believe they trust me."

She has been at various times in her life an actress, a painter, a collagist, a playwright, and a poet, each time baring herself to public criticism. In the late fifties she costarred with Ginger Rogers in an all-star television special of Noel Coward's *Tonight at 8:30,* acted opposite television star Gardner McKay in an episode of "Adventures in Paradise," and toured in Molnar's play *The Swan.* Her paintings have been exhibited, and a book of her collages has been published. She has written two plays, which are both under option but which have not been produced. In recent years Vanderbilt has achieved spectacular financial success, earning more money than she inherited, by signing a licensing agreement with Murjani International, which put her name on its line of jeans at the peak of the designer-jeans craze. The label reportedly took in $500 million a year, and Vanderbilt's face, in Murjani television commercials, became familiar to a whole new generation of Americans. She is also a designer of home furnishings, luggage, and handbags, all of which bear her name. Currently she is producing a perfume called Vanderbilt, which her business manager, Tom Andrews, claims is "far and away the biggest seller in American perfume." She has recently made her entry into the food area with Gloria Vanderbilt tofu glacé, a frozen dessert manufactured by the Dolly Madison company, and the Danbury Mint has just introduced the Gloria Vanderbilt bride doll, the first designer doll in its series. When I asked her which was better, inherited or earned wealth, she did not hesitate to reply, "Oh, darling, the money you make is better."

Copies of Wyatt Cooper's book, *Families: A Memoir and a Celebration,* are everywhere in her apartment. "Wyatt was the most extraordinary father," said Vanderbilt. "From the beginning, he treated our children as persons. It was everything I never had growing up." Everything she did not have as a child, in the way of love and family and emotional security, her sons by Cooper have had, and the affection that exists between mother and sons is evident. Carter is a sophomore at Princeton, and Anderson will graduate from the Dalton School in June. Last summer Anderson worked as a waiter at Mortimer's. "Of anything I have achieved in my life, really, to be the parent that I feel I am is for me the greatest thing that I could ever possibly achieve," she said.

When I asked her if she would ever remarry, she answered, "I tell you, it's seven years now since Wyatt has gone. It's only now that I'm really not numb. My boys are getting older. They're going to be really gone soon. And I would like to live with somebody. Now we don't have those pressures of getting married. But I'm not going to settle for anybody. I'm very, very fussy. Listen, in a strange way my book has become another person. I want to finish the other books, and all my direction is going toward that. But, of course, one wants to share things with one person."

It was time to go to lunch and give Bill Blass the cigarette case Noel Coward had once given Gertrude Lawrence. After that she had a meeting at Knopf to go over the final placement of the photographs in her book. The poor little rich girl of the thirties is very much in control of her life in the eighties. As she stood looking down on Gracie Square, a thought occurred to her, something Wannsie, her mother's maid for forty years, once said to her about the trial: "It was all a terrible misunderstanding."

Fatal Charm:
The Social Web of
Claus von Bülow

"THE PROBLEM with Claus," said one of Claus von Bülow's closest friends at a Park Avenue dinner party, "is that he does not dwell in the Palace of Truth. You see, he's a fake. He's always been a fake. His name is a fake. His life is a fake. He has created a character that he plays. Claus is trompe l'oeil."

"Come in, come in," said von Bülow expansively as he opened the front door to Helmut Newton, the photographer, who had just arrived from Monte Carlo for the session, and me. Von Bülow was standing in the marble-floored, green-walled, gilt-mirrored hallway of the Fifth Avenue apartment of his multimillionairess wife, whom he was accused of twice trying to kill. In the background a very old Chinese butler hovered, watching the master of the house usurp his duties. On that May Sunday of the seventh week of his second trial, the Danish society figure was dressed in tight blue jeans and a black leather jacket.

"This is the first time I've actually posed for a picture since my front and side shots," said von Bülow in his deep, resonant, English-school, international-set voice.

From the beginning, the von Bülow proceedings, legal and otherwise, had had an air of unreality about them. His once beautiful wife was one of the country's richest heiresses. His stepchildren were a prince and princess. His daughter was a disinherited teenager. His former mistress was a socialite actress. His current lady friend was a thrice-married Hungarian adventuress who was not the countess she was often described as being. The maid who testified against him had once worked for the Krupps. And lurking darkly in the background was a publicity-mad con man bent on destroying him.

The apartment of Sunny von Bülow, even by Fifth Avenue standards, is very grand. Located in one of the most exclusive buildings in New York, its current market value is estimated by one of the city's top realtors at nearly $8 million. Although a sophisticated friend of von Bülow's complained that the forty-foot drawing room has "far, far too many legs," it should be pointed out that the legs are by Chippendale and of museum quality, as is nearly every object in the fourteen-room apartment looking down on Central Park.

According to the terms of Sunny von Bülow's will, the apartment will go to von Bülow when she dies. So will Clarendon Court, the fabulous mansion set on ten acres overlooking the sea in Newport, Rhode Island, where her two comas took place during successive Christmas holidays, in 1979 and 1980. So will $14 million of her $75 million fortune. In the meantime the maintenance on the apartment is paid for by Sunny's estate, so in effect von Bülow and his self-proclaimed mistress, Andrea Reynolds, have been largely supported by his comatose wife since his conviction in 1982 for her attempted murder. That verdict was overturned on appeal because certain materials had been withheld from the defense and others had been improperly admitted as evidence.

"How is my old friend Bobby Moltke?" von Bülow asked Newton as he was setting up his photographic equipment. Then he added, "Not well, I hear." Newton resides in Monte Carlo, where Count Moltke lives part of the year, and the inquiry was distinctly perverse. Count Moltke is the father of

Alexandra Isles, von Bülow's former mistress, for whom, in the opinion of many, he sought to be rid of his wife. That day her name was prominent in the newspapers because another former lover of hers, the theater critic John Simon, had given an interview to the *New York Post* saying that he was in almost daily contact with the missing actress and that she had no intention of returning to testify at the second trial. Furthermore, Count Moltke, a Danish aristocrat, is known to loathe his fellow countryman for having involved the count's daughter in a scandal that has haunted her for years.

When I admired the carpet in the drawing room, von Bülow said, "I believe in building a room from the rug up. Did you ever know Billy Wallace in England? His father ordered this rug from Portugal before the war, and by the time it arrived the war had started, and it was put in storage and never used. I bought it from the family after the war." As usual, his attitude and conversation totally belied the fact that he was at that very moment a candidate for a long sojourn in one of Rhode Island's adult correctional institutions.

While von Bülow posed for Newton in front of a portrait of himself painted in Paris when he was twenty-one, Mrs. Reynolds, dressed in a white satin, lace-trimmed negligee, her eyes rimmed with black eyeliner, appeared and led me back to Sunny von Bülow's bedroom. On the bed Mrs. Reynolds had laid out evening dresses and a black leather outfit that matched von Bülow's for the shoot. One of the many stories about Andrea Reynolds that circulated at the trial in Providence and in the Upper East Side dining rooms of New York was that she wore Mrs. von Bülow's clothes and jewels, and that she had the clothes altered by a seamstress from the Yves Saint Laurent boutique on Madison Avenue.

"Not true!" Mrs. Reynolds had exclaimed when I mentioned these allegations a few days earlier. "I have far better jewels than Sunny von Bülow ever had. I've had fantastic jewels all my life. I wasn't even twenty when I had one of the biggest diamonds around. Be careful what you say about my jewels; I don't want to be robbed again."

She suffered a million-dollar jewel heist at her villa in Saint-Tropez in the late sixties, and was quoted then by the French columnist Jacques Chazot as saying, "They were only my *bijoux de plage.*" Another robbery occurred in her New York hotel suite while she was at the movies seeing *Deep Throat,* and once a pair of $80,000 earrings disappeared from a dressing room at Dior in Paris after she removed them to try on fur turbans. She suspects that they were lifted by an American-born duchess of historical importance who used the dressing room after her. She opened several velvet boxes on the bed, revealing a treasure trove of emeralds, diamonds, and pearls. "Mummy sent me these," she said.

During the final days of the first trial, Andrea Reynolds and her third husband, television producer Sheldon Reynolds, wrote a letter to von Bülow telling him they believed he was innocent. Lonely and isolated, von Bülow responded. They met in New York the day after his return there from Newport following the guilty verdict, and a warm friendship quickly developed. He spent weekends at the couple's country house in Livingston Manor, New York, and they stayed frequently at the von Bülow apartment. They made plans to have Reynolds be the agent for von Bülow's proposed autobiography and the miniseries based on it. (Von Bülow believes Robert Duvall should play him if a film or miniseries *is* ever made.) These plans fell apart when Reynolds, on a business trip in London, read in a gossip column that his wife and von Bülow were having an affair. A divorce is in progress. Mrs. Reynolds claims she was a neglected wife: "We were both unhappy when we met, Claus and I."

"Look," said one of von Bülow's swellest friends, who doesn't see him anymore, "six years ago, before all this happened, Claus wouldn't have had time for Andrea Reynolds." Although she claims to have known von Bülow for years, they did not travel in the same echelons of high society. She has a history of taking up with men who are at their low ebb and reviving them. A man just convicted of twice attempting to murder his wife would not seem like much of a catch to most women, but to Andrea Reynolds, Claus von Bülow, sentenced to thirty years pending appeal, was the ticket to center stage that she had always craved.

They made one of their first public appearances together in New York at a party given by Lady Jeanne Campbell, a former wife of Norman Mailer and the daughter of the eleventh Duke of Argyll. It was a glittering gathering of social names, literary names, titles, and a few film stars, and when von Bülow and Mrs. Reynolds entered late, after the theater, all conversation stopped. The occasion established Claus von Bülow's tremendous social celebrity; after that the couple maintained a high profile in the upper register of New York. They attended the opera regularly, on the smart night, and were frequent guests at the parties of such well-chronicled hostesses as von Bülow's old friend Mercedes Kellogg, the wife of Ambassador Francis Kellogg, and his new friend and staunch supporter Alice Mason, the New York realtor. They were also regulars at Mortimer's, the Upper East Side restaurant that caters to Manhattan's people-you-love-to-read-about.

Von Bülow inspires feelings that range from detestation to zealotry. At one of Alice Mason's parties, the editor of a magazine, appalled to be in the same room with a man found guilty of attempting to murder his wife, said she would leave if she were seated at the same table with him. Another woman at the party remarked, "He might look like the devil, but he's such a cozy old thing, and so amusing to sit next to at dinner. Have you seen him do his imitation of Queen Victoria?"

As a couple, they entertained frequently and elegantly at Sunny's Fifth Avenue apartment. "Very good food and lots of waiters," said man-about-town Johnny Galliher. One party was a *vernissage* for Andrea Reynolds's eyelift; the guest of honor was Dr. Daniel Baker, the plastic surgeon who had performed the operation. Their frantic pace continued right up to the second trial, and included an eighteenth-birthday party for Claus and Sunny's daughter, Cosima, at Mortimer's, attended by such *bon vivants* of New York as John Richardson, Kenny Lane, and Reinaldo and Carolina Herrera, but not by a single person of Cosima's age. "As long as they take Cosima with them when they go out, her trust pays the bill," said an informed source. They spent their last evening in New York before the second trial at a party given by Cornelia Guest, the city's most highly publicized postdebutante, whose mother, C. Z. Guest, the noted horsewoman, gardener, and socialite, was prepared to give testimony in von Bülow's behalf at the trial and corroborate the allegations of the late Truman Capote and others that Sunny von Bülow was a drug addict and a drunk.

For the first several weeks of the trial in Providence, my room at the Biltmore Plaza Hotel was on the same floor as the rooms von Bülow and Mrs. Reynolds shared. For several years I had seen the two of them around New York. Although we had never spoken, we had often been at the same parties or in the same restaurants. The first day in the courtroom, von Bülow recognized me but did not acknowledge me. The second day he nodded to me in the men's room. When we met in the corridor on the fourteenth floor of the hotel, he struck up a conversation about a portable word processor I was carrying. At that moment the door to their suite opened, and Andrea Reynolds came out into the hall.

She said to von Bülow, "I don't know Mr. Dunne's first name."

"Dominick," I said.

Von Bülow, leaning toward her, said slowly and deliberately, "And Mr. Dunne is not friendly toward us."

"I'm being friendly now," I said.

They invited me into their room, which had a sitting area at one end of it. An open closet was crammed with Mrs. Reynolds's clothes and at least twenty pairs of her shoes.

"We mustn't talk about the trial," said von Bülow.

For a while we talked about Cosima von Bülow, who had

that day been accepted at Brown University and would soon graduate from Brooks School in Massachusetts. Von Bülow spoke proudly and affectionately of her.

"Cosima has the best qualities of both her parents," said Andrea Reynolds. "She has the beauty and serenity of Sunny, and the intelligence and strength of Claus." Von Bülow acknowledged to me later Mrs. Reynolds's importance in Cosima's life. "She has been the adult woman to whom Cosima would constantly turn with her little flirtations or whatever a young girl wants to talk about. . . . No new woman in my life could have survived a lack of affinity with Cosima."

"Senator Pell called this morning and wanted to have lunch with Claus in Providence," said Andrea Reynolds, "and you can print that." She was referring to Senator Claiborne Pell of Rhode Island. "He obviously doesn't think he's guilty." Von Bülow remarked with the self-deprecatory kind of humor that had become a trademark with him, that he had declined the invitation because he didn't want to spoil the senator's chances of winning a sixth term by being seen with him in public.

That night I happened to fly back to New York on the same plane that Senator and Mrs. Pell were on. I struck up a conversation with Mrs. Pell and revealed that I was covering the von Bülow trial.

"I was with Claus von Bülow this afternoon and heard that the senator had called to ask him for lunch," I said.

"Is that what you were told?" Mrs. Pell asked. Nuala Pell is the daughter of Jo Hartford Bryce, the Great Atlantic & Pacific Tea Company heiress, and a Newport neighbor of the von Bülows.

"Yes," I replied.

"Mr. von Bülow called my husband. My husband didn't call Mr. von Bülow," she said.

Every Friday afternoon during the trial the von Bülow station wagon was packed and ready to depart the instant court adjourned. The doorman of the Biltmore Plaza Hotel held open the rear door, and the golden retriever, Tiger Lily, bolted into her regular place, eager to be gone. As Mrs. Reynolds, behind the wheel, waved gaily to photographers, von Bülow, wearing one of his handsomely cut cuffed-sleeved, foulard-lined tweed jackets, slipped into the front seat beside her, and they took off to New York. After the third week of the trial, they gave a christening party for Mrs. Reynolds's granddaughter, Eliza McCarthy. Von Bülow was the godfather, and the infant wore the christening dress Cosima had worn. Mrs. Reynolds, in a hat of red poppies with a veil and a blue high-fashion dress, nipped into Mortimer's for a celebratory drink between the religious service at St. Jean Baptiste Church and the seated lunch for twenty at the apartment: cold poached salmon, cucumber salad, and champagne, served by three waiters in addition to Tai, the Chinese butler.

Mrs. Reynolds interrupted von Bülow's toast to say, "Claus, Ann-Mari Bismarck is calling from London."

"Excuse me," said the host, leaving the table to talk with Princess von Bismarck, one of his strongest supporters.

"He's innocent," said the woman next to me. "It's those awful drugged-out children who have brought all this on and framed him. I can't sleep nights worrying about Claus."

A few days before the christening, von Bülow had gone with the jury, the judge, and both teams of lawyers for a view of Clarendon Court, the Newport mansion he and Sunny and their children had shared during the marriage. Clarendon Court was the location of the two alleged murder attempts. The gates leading to the courtyard of the Georgian mansion were boarded up to discourage passersby from snooping. Entering the grounds of his former home through a service entrance in a side wall, von Bülow broke down and cried, wiping away his tears with a silk handkerchief. Skeptics were quick to note that he was directly in line with a television camera raised high on a cherry picker to film what went on behind the walls, where the media were denied access.

"Why did you cry?" I asked him.

"It was the dogs," he replied, meaning three yellow Labradors that had belonged to him and Sunny and had often slept on their bed. "I remembered the dogs as young and lean, and they had become old and fat. But they remembered me, and they jumped up on me and greeted me, and I felt like Ulysses returning. And I broke down."

The only outward indication that Claus von Bülow was ever under severe strain was a habit he developed of stretching his neck and jutting out his chin at the same time, like a horse trying to throw the bit out of its mouth, or a man resisting a noose. Whatever one felt personally about the guilt or innocence of the man, one could not deny his charm, which was enormous, in a European, upper-class, courtly sort of way. One of the first calls he made after his arrest was to John Aspinall, his English gambler friend, to say that, alas, he would not be able to attend the ball Aspinall and his wife were giving that weekend in Kent.

The slightest incident would trigger an inexhaustible supply of heavy-furniture anecdotes about the titled, the famous, and the wealthy—his standard points of reference. He would regale you with the fact that Christian VII of Denmark, whose portrait hangs in his drawing room, died of syphilis and drink. Or that the marble of his dining table, as blue as malachite is green, is called azurite. "I hate malachite, don't you?" he asked. "It reminds me of the fellow who was so proud of his malachite cuff links until a Russian grand duke said to him, 'Ah, yes, I used to have a staircase made of that.' " Once when a waiter poured him wine, he sniffed it, sipped it, savored it, nodded his approval of it, and then continued with the anecdote he was telling about the Dowager Marchioness of Dufferin and Ava, concerning Sunny von Bülow's maid, Maria Schrallhammer, who testified against him in both trials. " 'I know how difficult it is to get a good maid,' Maureen said, 'but this is ridiculous.' "

He would cite as his Newport supporters Alan Pryce-Jones, Oatsie Charles, Mr. and Mrs. John Winslow, and especially Anne Brown, the septuagenarian dowager Mrs. John Nicholas Brown, born a Kinsolving, who took the stand in von Bülow's behalf as a character witness at the first trial and became his most devoted champion in the deeply divided summer colony. At a dinner in Palm Beach last winter given by Mr. and Mrs. Walter Gubelmann, also of Newport, Mrs. Brown announced that her faith in Claus von Bülow remained undiminished, and she asked the other guests to raise their glasses in a toast to him. No one rose to join her.

Von Bülow continued to wear the wedding ring from his marriage to Sunny, although he said any number of times that they would have divorced if what happened had not happened. The ring was in fact returned to him before the first trial by Alexandra Isles, his former mistress, whose appearance at that trial helped to convict him and whose melodramatic appearance at the second trial again turned sentiment against him. Mrs. Isles had had the wedding ring in her possession because it embarrassed her to have him wear it during the course of their affair.

Sometimes he spoke of Sunny as if she were a beloved late wife. "That was one of Sunny's favorite books," he said one day when he saw me reading *The Raj Quartet* during a break in the jury selection. Another time, at the apartment on Fifth Avenue, he saw me looking at a silver-framed photograph of her, taken by Horst. "God, she was beautiful," he said quietly.

"Were you ever in love with Sunny?" I asked.

"Oh, yes. Very much so," he replied in his dark baritone. "I'm really not letting out any secrets when I say that Sunny and I were geographically apart, but in every other sense together, for two years before we got married."

Who exactly is Claus von Bülow? For most of his life, dark rumors have circulated about him: that he was a page boy at Hermann Göring's wedding, that he is a necrophiliac, that he killed his mother and kept her body on ice, that he was involved in international espionage. Von Bülow either has a logical explanation for each rumor or shrugs it off as ludicrous.

The necrophilia story, he says, was pinned on him in 1949, as a joke, on Capri, by Fiat owner Gianni Agnelli and Prince Dado Ruspoli. "Like dirt, it stuck," he says.

He was born Claus Cecil Borberg on August 11, 1926, in Copenhagen to Jonna and Svend Borberg, who divorced when he was four. His mother was a beauty who throughout her life developed strong friendships with men in high places. His father was a drama critic who greatly admired the Germans, even after they occupied Denmark in World War II. "He gave a good name to a bad cause," says von Bülow about his father. "He dined with the wrong people." After the war he was arrested as a collaborator and sentenced to four years in prison. Von Bülow says that his father's conviction—like his own thirty-six years later—was thrown out on appeal, and he was released after eighteen months. However, when von Bülow returned to Denmark, he did not go to see his father, who died broken and ostracized a year after his release.

His mother was residing in England at the time of the German invasion of Denmark. Claus was spirited there via Sweden in the early years of the war through the efforts of both his parents. Claus took the name of his maternal grandfather, Frits Bülow, a former minister of justice, since the name Borberg had been besmirched. The *von* was added later.

When he was sixteen, he was accepted at Cambridge University, from which he graduated in 1946 with a law degree. Too young to take the bar, he spent a year in Paris auditing courses at the Ecole des Sciences Politiques and introducing himself to the world of international high society. After working with Hambros bank in London, he joined the law offices of Quintin Hogg, later Lord Hailsham. An interesting fact that was not brought up in either trial is that during the 1950s his law firm handled the first known case of murder by insulin injection.

Von Bülow and his mother, with whom he lived until her death, bought one of the grandest apartments in London, in Belgrave Square, which, von Bülow says, "dined two hundred with ease and slept three with difficulty." Before gambling became legal, he rented it out to his friend John Aspinall for private gambling parties. He also made friends with Lord Lucan who later murdered his children's nanny in the mistaken belief that she was his wife, and whose subsequent whereabouts have never been ascertained. Tall and handsome, with an eye for the right social contacts, von Bülow soon knew all the people who mattered. In Saint Moritz he had an affair with socialite Ann Woodward after she killed her husband.

In the early sixties, when he was thirty-three years old, von Bülow was hired as an administrative assistant to the legendary oil tycoon J. Paul Getty, who had recently moved his headquarters of the Los Angeles-based company to London. There has been much speculation as to exactly what von Bülow's importance was in the Getty empire, whether he was an errand boy or a figure of consequence. Getty hated to fly, so von Bülow frequently represented him at meetings and reported back to him. A woman friend of Getty's told me that von Bülow arranged parties in his apartment at which the old man could meet girls. What is certain is that his income from working for one of the richest men in the world was less than $20,000 a year. Von Bülow speaks of Mr. Getty with enormous affection and says that one of the major mistakes of his life was leaving England and that job.

Margaret, Duchess of Argyll, was a great friend of Paul Getty's and often served as hostess at his parties. She remembers one occasion when she returned to London from Getty's estate in Surrey with von Bülow, whom she did not know well at the time. She was then involved in one of the most scandalous divorces in English history. Von Bülow asked her if she knew that her husband had taken a room at the Ritz in London that connected with the room of a certain Mrs. So-and-so. She did not know. "But, you can imagine, it was very important information for me to have at that time," said the duchess, "and Mr. von Bülow didn't even know the duke."

In 1966 von Bülow married the American Princess Martha "Sunny" Crawford von Auersperg, thirteen months after her divorce from her first husband, Prince Alfie von Auersperg, on whom she had settled a million dollars and two houses. Tired of living in Austria, tired of her husband's philandering, tired of big-game hunting in Africa, Sunny wanted to bring up her two children from that marriage, Princess Annie-Laurie von Auersperg and Prince Alexander von Auersperg, aged seven and six, in the United States. Fifteen years later those same two children would charge their stepfather with attempting to murder her. The couple settled in New York in Sunny's apartment at 960 Fifth Avenue, the same apartment where von Bülow and Mrs. Reynolds reside.

A year later, their only child, Cosima, was born. Prince Otto von Bismarck, J. Paul Getty, the Marchioness of Londonderry, and Isabel Glover were her godparents.

"Did you see yourself on Dan Rather last night?" I asked Andrea Reynolds the morning after CBS had run a long sequence of the trial, showing her watching Alexandra Isles, von Bülow's mistress before her, testify against him.

"No, darling, I didn't know it was on. But so many people have been filming me—can you imagine if I spent my days seeing if I can see myself on TV? How did I look?"

Clearly the star of the second trial was Mrs. Reynolds, although she was, much to her chagrin, not allowed to sit in the courtroom. She was here, there, and everywhere else, though, known to every employee in the Biltmore Plaza Hotel, to all the cabdrivers of Providence, and to each member of the press. Forty-eight years old, she was born in Hungary and raised and educated in Switzerland. She speaks seven languages. Vivacious, curvaceous, and flirtatious, she seems a sort of latter-day Gabor, with a determination factor somewhere on the scale between Imelda Marcos and Leona Helmsley. She was openly loathed by Claus von Bülow's lawyers long before she told a reporter from *People* magazine that the jury didn't like Thomas Puccio: "They draw away from him when he approaches the jury box." Puccio, von Bülow's tough defense attorney, gained national recognition as the Abscam prosecutor. Friends claim Mrs. Reynolds knew more about the first trial than the lawyers did. One reporter counted twenty-nine pages of Sunny von Bülow's medical records spread out on tables and chairs in her suite.

She was Claus von Bülow's most passionate defender, fighting to vindicate her man and at the same time establishing a name for herself. It was she, according to Sheldon Reynolds, who got most of the affidavits from prominent people saying that Sunny von Bülow was an alcoholic. Von Bülow said about her, "I realize that that Hungarian hussar has, often to one's total exhaustion, whipped everybody, including me, into activity." Nowhere was this more evident than in von Bülow's dealings with the media.

During the first trial, in Newport, von Bülow sometimes spoke to members of the press in the corridors of the courthouse during recesses, but he never socialized with them. During the second trial, in Providence, with Mrs. Reynolds at the helm, he openly courted the media with masterly manipulation. They were on a first-name basis with most of the members, dined regularly with them in the various restaurants of Providence, and drove at least one reporter to New York in their station wagon for the weekend, dazzling them all, or so they thought, with their glamour, while always stipulating that anything they said was strictly off the record. Mrs. Reynolds often telephoned reporters if she didn't like the way they reported on the trial, and occasionally went over their heads to their editors. When Tony Burton wrote in the *New York Daily News* that while the jury was sequestered in the Holiday Inn, cut off from family and friends, the defendant and his lady friend were dining nightly in the best restaurants in Providence, Mrs. Reynolds called him a Commie pinko faggot. Eventually reporters grew sick of the off-the-record quotes fed to them by the pair. One journalist baited Mrs. Reynolds by asking her, "Come on, Andrea, what kind of fuck is Claus?" She replied, without a second's hesitation, "How can you expect me to answer that? If I tell you he's good, there will be even more women after him than there already are, and if I tell you he's no good, how does that make me look?"

Barred from the courtroom, Mrs. Reynolds watched the trial in the truck of Cable News Network, which carried the proceedings live, gavel to gavel. There she was able to see exactly what went on in the courtroom, without all the commercials and cutaways. To the dismay of the CNN personnel, she slowly began to take over the small booth. When Alexander von Auersperg's lawyer entered one day, he was met by Mrs. Reynolds. When Judge Corinne Grande called the booth, Mrs. Reynolds answered the telephone. Mrs. Reynolds was then asked not to return. She begged to be readmitted for just one more day in order to watch a hearing for one of several mistrials requested by the defense, but CNN declined. "Even a maid gets two weeks' notice," snapped Mrs. Reynolds.

Mrs. Reynolds's style was a curious mixture of femininity and rough language. Her stories about the von Auersperg children, whom she had never met, were scurrilous. "Everyone who ever went to Xenon knows all about them," she said. On a secret tape submitted to the producers of "60 Minutes," she referred to Alexander as an asshole.

One day I asked her, "Is it true that you shot your first husband?"

"Absolutely not."

"That's a pretty well circulated story about you, Andrea."

"It wasn't my first husband. It was my second husband," she said. "And I didn't shoot him. He shot himself. When I left him. I'm the one who saved him. Not the one who shot him."

Andrea Reynolds was born Andrea Milos. Her family was described to me by a Hungarian who knew them as noble without a title. She and her mother fled Hungary for Switzerland when the Russians arrived, but her father, a banker, was forced to stay behind. Eventually he escaped to Morocco with the family jewels, sewn, according to Mrs. Reynolds, into the seams of his lederhosen. In Casablanca, he opened a dry-cleaning establishment called Mille Fleurs, and his fortune started to flourish again after he secured the business of the United States Army base in Casablanca. After her parents divorced, her mother married Sir Oliver Duncan, an immensely rich Englishman with pro-German leanings who sat out the war in Switzerland. Older by far than his new wife and suffering from Parkinson's disease, he was an heir to the Pfizer pharmaceutical company. The facts of his death are murky, but nearly all sources agree that he was kidnapped from Switzerland and hidden in a convent in Rome. At some point during his incarceration, he was carried to Monte Carlo and forced to sign away his fortune to his abductors. Some Europeans familiar with the story told me his body had never been found, but Mrs. Reynolds said she knew exactly where her stepfather was buried and that his funeral was attended by hundreds of prominent people. Her mother, the widowed Lady Duncan, now lives in Brazil. "During all these topsy-turvy things, I always went to the best schools," said Mrs. Reynolds.

Her first husband was a French-Italian named Ellis Giorgini. They had, according to Mrs. Reynolds, "a beautiful wedding in Paris." But the marriage was short-lived: "He drank a bit too much." Her second husband, Pierre Frottier-Duche, a Frenchman, is the father of her only child, Caroline, who is a student of veterinary medicine at the University of Pennsylvania and the mother of Eliza McCarthy. They lived in a house in Paris that had once belonged to Anatole France, and had a villa in Saint-Tropez. At one time very rich, Frottier suffered severe financial reverses. When he later went bankrupt, Mrs. Reynolds gave him back all the jewels he had given her. "I'm a gentleman," she said. Asked to comment on the story that Frottier had been forced to become a taxi driver after he went broke, she replied, "No, no, no, a limousine driver, and he would pick up people like Henry Ford, whom he knew from before, and Henry would sit up in the front seat with him when he realized it was Pierre."

Her conversation is peppered with fashionable names. The

late Florence Gould, daughter-in-law of robber baron Jay Gould, was the godmother of her daughter, Caroline. The late Babe Paley was the matron of honor at her third marriage, to film producer Sheldon Reynolds. When pressed, she admitted, "Well, actually, Babe was sick on the day of the wedding, with a toothache, and someone else had to stand in, but I think of her as my matron of honor."

She claims to be on excellent terms with all her husbands, but at least one did not share this opinion. "If Claus has to marry Andrea," said Sheldon Reynolds, "he will wish he'd been convicted."

One night the telephone rang in my hotel room in Providence. It was Mrs. Reynolds. She asked me not to mention something she had told me about her first husband, and I agreed not to.

"I talk too much when I'm with you," she said. "I'm going to have to arrange for you to have a little accident."

We both laughed and hung up.

A rich person on trial is very different from an ordinary person on trial. The powerful defense team assembled by von Bülow for the second trial so outshone the prosecution that the trial often seemed like a football game between the New York Jets and Providence High. Outsiders versed in legal costs estimated that the second trial alone cost von Bülow somewhere in the neighborhood of a million dollars. Besides Thomas Puccio and Alan Dershowitz, the Harvard law professor who won the appeal, four other lawyers, two of them from New York, attended the trial daily. Von Bülow even hired his own court stenographer, because the court-appointed one could not turn out transcripts fast enough to suit the defense. That cost alone, combined with printing, binding, and messenger fees, was probably close to $1,500 a day. Where the money for this extravagant operation came from was anyone's guess. Von Bülow's personal income is $120,000 a year, the interest on a $2 million trust Sunny von Bülow donated to the Metropolitan Opera with the stipulation that the income should go to von Bülow for life. Some said he sold art objects. Others said he had a loan of $900,000 from the Getty Oil Company. Still others said Mrs. Reynolds controlled the backers who provided the money.

"Are you in love with Andrea?" I asked von Bülow one Sunday morning late in the trial, when we were sitting on a bench in Central Park.

His eyes were closed. He was catching the warm May rays of the sun on his face. "I love Andrea," he replied slowly, measuring his words. "I find this very hard. Being *in* love is very different from loving somebody. There has to be the right timing and the right climate. . . . The climate and timing are wrong. I just don't have enough left for the enthusiasm and recklessness and carefreeness that is inherent in falling in love. I'm a man with a noose around my neck."

David Marriott was meticulously suited and vested in beige gabardine, with an M monogrammed on his French cuffs. Tall, slender, twenty-seven years old, he had arrived for our meeting, as he arrived for all of his public appearances, in a limousine. His chauffeur-bodyguard sat with us in the cocktail lounge of the Biltmore Plaza, munching peanuts.

"Would you describe the color of your glasses as grape?"

"No, rose. The press always calls them rose. Call them rose. Not grape," insisted David Marriott.

One of the most bizarre and unresolved aspects of the complicated von Bülow story was this mysterious young man from Wakefield, Massachusetts, where he lived with his mother. David Marriott had a voracious appetite for publicity and a deep hatred of Claus von Bülow and Andrea Reynolds. He surfaced after the first trial and was, for some time, embraced by von Bülow, Mrs. Reynolds, and Alan Dershowitz. Because of Marriott, von Bülow announced that he had discovered dramatic new evidence which he claimed would establish his innocence. At the urging of a later discredited Catholic priest, Father Philip Magaldi, Marriott swore that he had delivered packages containing hypodermic needles, bags of white powder, syringes, vials of Demerol, and pills to Alexander von Auersperg, who had told him that some of the material was for his mother, "to keep her off my back."

This evidence was a direct contradiction of the state's claim that the only person in the von Bülow household who had access to, or familiarity with, drugs and drug paraphernalia was Claus von Bülow. Affidavits signed by both Marriott and Father Magaldi were therefore important to von Bülow for his appeal.

Marriott paid visits to von Bülow's Fifth Avenue apartment and to the Reynoldses' country house in Livingston Manor, had lunches and dinners in fashionable restaurants, and took several trips to Puerto Rico, paid for by von Bülow. But then a falling-out occurred. By the start of the second trial, Marriott had recanted his original confession, and was claiming instead that his story had been concocted by von Bülow and that the drugs and needles he had delivered "didn't go to Sunny and Alex, they went to Claus." Marriott further revealed that he had secreted a tape recorder in his Jockey shorts and taped von Bülow, Mrs. Reynolds, Father Magaldi, and Alan Dershowitz in compromising conversations. He invited members of the press to his house in Wakefield to listen to them. Although the voices of von Bülow, Mrs. Reynolds, and Father Magaldi were distinguishable, the content of their talk, while suspicious in nature, was not incriminating. That left Marriott unwanted by either side.

Marriott was variously described by the media as an undertaker, a male prostitute, and a drug dealer. He claimed to me to be none of these, although he said that von Bülow had once offered to send him to mortician's school, and his remarks about von Bülow were filled with homosexual innuendo. Von Bülow said he had never heard of David Marriott before he came forward with his story of having sold drugs at Clarendon Court. Marriott, on the other hand, said he had known von Bülow for seven or eight years, having met him through a now deceased twenty-three-year-old drug dealer and hustler named Gilbert Jackson, who was, in Marriott's words, "bound up in elastic cord and strangled and stabbed many, many times on August 28, 1978." Two vagrants are serving time for that murder. When I asked Andrea Reynolds whether von Bülow ever knew Gilbert Jackson, she said, "Darling, one doesn't know people like that."

In a move of desperation to achieve the notoriety that was eluding him, Marriott passed out defamatory leaflets about his onetime cohort, Father Magaldi, during mass at St. Anthony Church in North Providence, but the local television stations, alerted by Marriott of his intentions to make scandalous allegations about the priest, ignored the stunt.

When I called Marriott to double-check his version of how he had met von Bülow, he said, "I'm not telling you this unless I get paid for it. I'm saving that for my book."

"Listen, it doesn't matter, I'm running short of space anyway. I don't need to use you at all."

"It's all right. You can use it. I met him through Gilbert Jackson in 1978."

During the seventh week of the trial, David Marriott was severely beaten up. His nose was broken and his eyes were blackened. No explanation was given for the assault.

After the jury retired to deliberate, Father Magaldi was indicted for perjury and conspiring to obstruct justice by lying in behalf of Claus von Bülow.

Our mother, as you may know, has been in an irreversible coma for four years: she cannot see, hear or speak. She is a victim in every sense. Our mother gave us unfailing love and devotion. She taught us the very big difference between right and wrong. We carry her sensitivities and her teachings as, perhaps, only children can. . . . She was not there to tell what had happened to her. She was not there to speak for herself when her character was assaulted. Lying in a deep coma, our mother became a non-person.

That is a portion of a letter written by Alexander von Auersperg and Annie-Laurie Kneissl that appeared in the newsletter of an organization known as Justice for Surviving Victims,

Inc. Alexander and Annie-Laurie, who is known as Ala, remained remote figures throughout most of the second trial, but then they emerged in a blaze of worldwide publicity at a press conference in which they begged their stepfather's former mistress, Alexandra Isles, who had fled the country, to come forward and provide critical testimony. "We realize that coming forward the last time was an act of courage on your part. We ask that you summon the same courage again."

Sunny's children by her first marriage, backed by their maternal grandmother, Annie-Laurie Aitken, who died last year, undertook the original investigation of their stepfather and hired former New York District Attorney Richard Kuh to confirm their suspicions. Jonathan Houston, executive director of Justice Assistance in Providence, brought me together with Ala Kneissl early in the trial. We met for the first time in the New York apartment of Pamela Combemale, a close friend of Sunny von Bülow's and the cousin of another ill-fated heiress, Barbara Hutton.

Married to an Austrian, the beautiful Ala Kneissl was pregnant with her second child when we met. Her brother, who is equally good-looking, graduated from Brown University in 1983 and works in the retirement division of E. F. Hutton. Deeply devoted to their mother, they acknowledged that she and von Bülow were happy for many years, and that they themselves had had affection for him. They had called him Uncle Claus or Ducky. Why Ducky? In those days, while his hair transplant was growing in, he wore a toupee, and when he swam he held his head far out of the water like a duck. Their mother, they said, preferred home life to social life, and they reminisced about family meals and going to films together and lying on their mother's bed watching television.

While the jury was out deliberating, Ala and Alexander invited me to Newport to spend the night at Clarendon Court. We dined across Bellevue Avenue at the home of the Countess Elizabeth de Ramel, an American friend of Ala's, titled by a former marriage, whose Newport antecedents, the Prince and Wood-Prince families, date back for generations.

There were a dozen guests. Despite attempts at joviality, the conversation throughout dinner never strayed far from the trial and the looming verdict. Ala and Alexander, who were dubbed "the kids" by the press during the trial, are remarkably unspoiled for young people who have grown up amid a kind of wealth and opulence that is almost incomprehensible.

Clarendon Court faces Bellevue Avenue on one side and the Atlantic Ocean on the other. In 1956 it was used as the setting for Grace Kelly's home in the film *High Society*. Another page of its colorful history concerns a young man named Paul Molitor, who was hired by Claus von Bülow in 1979 from the China Trade Museum in Massachusetts to work for the Newport Preservation Society, of which von Bülow was then an officer. Molitor beat out 120 other applicants for the job. Shortly after his arrival in Newport, von Bülow invited him to move into the carriage house on the grounds of Clarendon Court. Extremely personable, he soon became a popular extra man at dinner parties. He was in residence at the time of Sunny von Bülow's second coma, and his Newport friends recall that he was extremely fearful of having to testify at the first trial. He was not called to the stand, but one night six months later, he jumped off the Newport Bridge. A persistent rumor in the resort colony is that he was pushed. He was wearing a dinner jacket. An early report in the *Providence Journal*, later denied, said that his feet were bound with chicken wire.

Clarendon Court is a house where you walk through huge rooms to get to other huge rooms. Outside, between the terrace and the sea, is the mammoth swimming pool built by Sunny when she acquired the house after her second marriage; two fountains in the pool shoot water twenty feet into the air. She gave her last great party here, a twenty-first-birthday celebration for Alexander, at which all the guests wore white and played croquet on the sweeping lawns as the mist rolled in from the ocean.

"That was Claus's," said Ala, with a shudder of distaste, pointing to a cast-iron jardiniere held up by three mythological figures with erect penises. Some of the furniture in the house belongs to von Bülow, from his Belgrave Square apartment. At the end of the first trial, when he put in a list of the pieces of furniture that were his, he claimed a partners' desk. Later it was discovered in an old photograph that the desk had been in Sunny's house in Kitzbühel during her marriage to Alfie von Auersperg. The furniture in von Bülow's study has a different feeling entirely from the rest of the house; exotic formula-laden pieces crowd the room, and opium pipes hang on the wall. It was here that he left the note containing the phrase "metal box," which led to the discovery of the infamous black bag that contained the syringe and insulin that were at the heart and soul of the case.

In a world of people who call their mother Mummy, Ala and Alexander call theirs Mom. As I walked through the house with them, they said things like "This was my mom's favorite color," pointing to the coral-painted walls of an upstairs sitting room, or "You should have seen my mom arrange flowers."

Their mother's bedroom remains exactly the way it was on the night of the second coma. Her elegantly canopied bed consists of two beds pushed together, made up separately with Porthault sheets and monogrammed blanket covers. On von Bülow's side of the bed is an old, silver-framed photograph of him in a striking, almost noble pose. I opened a handsome box on his bed table. It was filled with cartridge shells. Under the shells was a used syringe. In one of Sunny's closets, next to her evening dresses, are unopened gifts from that last Christmas of 1980—one from her lifelong friend Isabel Glover, another from her now deceased mother. Their festive wrappings are faded and limp.

On the day that Alexandra Isles returned to the United States to testify against von Bülow, Cosima graduated from Brooks School. She was the only member of the graduating class with no relatives present, but her classmates rallied behind her and cheered loudly when she received her diploma.

The estrangement from her half brother and half sister was

over Clarendon Court. Although she was welcome to use the house at any time, Ala and Alexander would not vacate the place for her. When I told von Bülow that Ala and Alexander still cared for Cosima, he replied, "I just think they have to put their money where their mouth is. I am not impressed with constant repetitions of love and holding on to her money. I'd much rather hear them say they hate the brat and that's why they're holding on to her money."

Both von Bülow and Mrs. Reynolds were obsessed with the fact that Cosima had been cut out of the $110 million estate of her grandmother, Annie-Laurie Aitken, for siding with her father. "She's out twenty-five million," Mrs. Reynolds said to me one day after Cosima and her boyfriend had left the table at Mortimer's.

One of the most poignant moments of the trial occurred on the last day, when all three of Sunny von Bülow's children appeared in the courthouse. It was the first time Ala and Cosima had seen each other since a chance encounter on the street three years earlier. As the divided family passed in the corridor, they looked straight ahead and did not speak. "She's gotten so beautiful," Ala said to me later of Cosima. "My mother would be very proud of her."

No one else in the trial came near to the sheer dramatic power of Alexandra Isles. Often described in the media as a soap-opera actress, the patrician Mrs. Isles attended the same schools as Sunny von Bülow: Chapin and St. Timothy's. Her mother, the Countess Mab Moltke, was born into the Wilson family of San Francisco, whose fortune, diminished now, traces its roots back to the Comstock lode. Mrs. Isles is divorced from Philip Isles, a member of the wealthy Lehman banking family; his father changed his name from Ickelheimer in the 1950s. Following their divorce, Isles married the former wife of Dr. Richard Raskind, who changed his name to Renée Richards when he became a woman.

Deeply wounded by the hostile reaction she received at the end of the first trial, von Bülow's former mistress fled the country rather than testify again, believing, she said, that a videotape of her testimony in the first trial could be used in the second. At a New York party, Mrs. Isles's friend John Simon told me that under no condition would she return. He claimed, and later repeated to the press, that she did not want her son, Adam, fifteen, a student at Groton, to suffer the embarrassment of having his mother on the stand as the mistress and motive of the defendant in an attempted-murder trial; that her mother was ill and had begged her not to take the stand; that she was terrified of being cross-examined by Thomas Puccio, because she knew von Bülow's lawyer would expose her private life; and that she had received threatening letters from von Bülow warning her not to testify. Von Bülow vehemently and angrily denied this, claiming he had not been in touch with her since the first trial.

Mrs. Isles, who was reported to be hiding out at Forest Mere, an exclusive fat farm in England, flew from Frankfurt, Germany, the day after the von Auersperg children made their plea for her to return. After conferring with the prosecution team in Boston, she spent the night under an assumed name in the Ritz-Carlton Hotel, watching a Celtics game with her son. The next morning she testified that von Bülow had called her at her mother's house in Ireland after the first coma to say that he had lain on the bed next to his wife for hours waiting for her to die, but that at the last minute he had not been able to go through with it and had called the doctor. Feisty and unwavering, she withstood the pummeling of Thomas Puccio. When he asked her to explain how she could have continued an affair with a man she suspected of trying to kill his wife, she shouted, "Have you ever been in love?" Then she added, "I doubt it."

Mrs. Reynolds was openly contemptuous of Mrs. Isles. Speaking of the jury, she said to me, "They have been told Claus was consumed by so much passion he was willing to kill his wife and get her money so that he could marry Alexandra Isles. In real life, two days after the end of the first trial, he and I fell in love with each other." Later the press said that she bared her claws and declared that Alexandra Isles had had two or three men at a time. Mrs. Isles had no comment to make about Mrs. Reynolds.

Meanwhile, the subject, or object, of all this conflict, Sunny von Bülow, lies in the sixth year of her coma on the tenth floor of the Harkness Pavilion in the Columbia-Presbyterian Medical Center in New York City. She is not, as many believe, on a life-support system, nor is she the total vegetable she is often described as being. I was told that the yearly cost of maintaining her is considerably in excess of half a million dollars. Her $725-a-day room is guarded around the clock by a special security force, and private nurses and a maid look after her at all times. A maze of curtained screens further protects her from the remote possibility that an outsider should gain entry to her room. A current photograph of the comatose woman would be worth a fortune.

Dr. Richard Stock, who has been her physician for twenty-nine years, as he was her mother's and grandmother's, visits her several times a week. She is fed through a tube in her nose. She receives physical therapy and dental care, and her hair is washed and set twice a week. Her own skin creams are used on her hands and face. She wears her own nightgowns and bed jackets and sleeps on Porthault sheets. Music plays in the room, and there are always highly scented flowers on her bedside table.

Ala and Alexander visit her regularly. Sometimes Ala brings her two-year-old daughter, also called Sunny, so that her mother can know she has a grandchild. They talk to her. They touch her. They tell her about things.

In a bizarre twist of fate, their father, Prince Alfie von Auersperg, is also in an irreversible coma, in Salzburg, the result of an automobile accident two years ago, when he was driving with Alexander. Their father's sister, Princess Hetty von Auersperg von Bohlen, the wife of Arndt von Bohlen and Halbach, the Krupp munitions heir, has found a healer in Europe who specializes in comas. She plans to bring the healer to New York to minister to her former sister-in-law.

There are those who say that when Alfie von Auersperg and Sunny von Bülow stood side by side in the receiving line at their daughter's marriage to Franz Kneissl, he asked her to divorce Claus von Bülow and remarry him.

Maria Schrallhammer, the German maid so devoted to her mistress that she refused to divulge to two sets of defense attorneys the fact that Sunny von Bülow had had a face-lift because she had promised her she would never tell, also visits regularly, as does G. Morris Gurley, the Chemical Bank trust officer for Sunny's estate. Old friends are occasionally admitted, and one of them told me, "She has a personality just like you or I do. She reacts differently to different people. Some days you have a termagant on your hands. You try to brush her hair and you will have hell to pay. Other times, if the shades aren't open, she still looks beautiful in the half-light, although her hair has gone completely gray."

Cosima von Bülow has not been to the hospital since December 1981. Nor has Claus von Bülow.

In the three years that preceded Sunny von Bülow's second coma, most of her friends did not see her, or saw her only rarely. Some of them claim that von Bülow isolated her, answered the telephone for her, took messages that they felt she never received.

One of Sunny's last public appearances in New York was at the funeral of her childhood friend Peggy Bedford, a Standard Oil heiress with an inheritance comparable to Sunny's, although she was reputed to have gone through most of it by the time of her death in an automobile accident. Married first to Thomas Bancroft, she had later become the Princess d'Arenberg and then the Duchess d'Uzes. Friends say they spoke with Sunny on the steps of St. James Church following the service and found her warm and friendly and eager to make plans to see them. Then von Bülow appeared at her side, took hold of her by the elbow, and led her off to their waiting limousine. One old friend, Diego Del Vayo, remembers that she waved a gloved hand to him out of the car window.

•　　•　　•

For the eight weeks that the trial mesmerized the country, a
related development of the strange case ran its parallel course.
Nowhere was the scent of rot more pervasive than in the
minimally publicized story of a Providence parish priest, Father Philip Magaldi, and his onetime companion David Marriott, an unemployed mystery man who drove around in
limousines and who was happy to show anyone who cared to
look Xeroxed copies of his hotel bills from Puerto Rican resorts, which he claimed were paid for by Claus von Bülow.
Why, people wondered, if von Bülow was innocent, would
he have involved himself in such an unsavory atmosphere?

Let us backtrack.

On July 21, 1983, Father Magaldi, on the stationery of
Saint Anthony Church, 5 Gibbs Street, North Providence,
Rhode Island, wrote and signed the following statement in
the presence of a notary:

> TO WHOM IT MAY CONCERN:
> . . . I wish to state that I am ready to testify, if necessary, and
> under oath, that DAVID MARRIOTT did in fact discuss with me
> in professional consultation, his delivering to Mr. Claus von Bü-
> low's stepson, Alexander [von Auersperg], packages which he
> thought contained drapery materials from his friend Gilbert [Jack-
> son] in Boston, but on one occasion a package which he opened
> contained drugs which were delivered to the Newport mansion and
> accepted by Mrs. Sunny von Bülow who stated Alexander was not
> home but she had been expecting the package.
>
> My reason for writing this affidavit is that in the event of acci-
> dent or death, I wish to leave testimony as to the veracity of the
> statements made to me by DAVID MARRIOTT and also that as
> his counselor in spiritual matters, I advised him to inform Mr.
> Claus von Bülow and his lawyers as to what he knew concerning
> drug involvement by Alexander. I intend to speak to Mr. Roberts,
> the Attorney General of the State of Rhode Island, concerning
> these matters in August.

Five days later, on white watermarked stationery bearing
the engraved address 960 Fifth Avenue, New York, New

York, Claus von Bülow wrote Father Magaldi a letter that was quoted in the *New York Post* by gossip columnist Cindy Adams at the conclusion of the second trial. It reads in part:

Dear Father Magaldi:

I want to thank you for your kindness and courage in braving the storm and the airport delays, and then coming to meet me in New York. Had I been able to contact you in Boston I would gladly have faced those problems myself.

We were however rewarded with a very enjoyable evening, and I am grateful to you.

I want to repeat my wish to consult with you in finding an acceptable charity for donating the royalties of my book. The total profits, including film rights, could be anything between $500,000 and $1,000,000. . . . I will be happy to meet with you in Providence, Boston, or New York at your convenience.

On September 30, 1983, Father Magaldi, in a document notarized by his attorney, William A. Dimitri, Jr. (who later became the attorney for von Bülow's mistress, Andrea Reynolds), made the following statement:

In addition to my affidavit I wish to state something which I feel is too delicate a matter to come before the media and public at this time.

I refer to pictures shown me by David Marriott in which Alexander is engaged in homosexual activity with an unidentified male whom David told me was Gilbert Jackson.

Because these pictures in my estimation served no purpose and were patently pornographic, I destroyed them. However I can state that I recognized Alexander in the picture but cannot verify that the other was Gilbert Jackson since I have never seen him.

In actuality, Father Magaldi had never met Alexander von Auersperg, and Alexander von Auersperg had never met Gilbert Jackson, who was murdered in 1978, and therefore no such pornographic pictures ever existed for Father Magaldi to destroy. In other, more exotic areas of his life, Father Magaldi traveled in the netherland of Boston under the alias Paul Marino. It was in this role that he met David Marriott, in the Greyhound bus terminal in 1977, and not in the spiritual capacity he claimed in his affidavit. David Marriott told me that he did not know his benefactor was a Catholic priest until Magaldi was in a minor automobile accident several years after their friendship began and his true identity came out.

Marriott, who participated in preparing these and other affidavits besmirching the names of Claus von Bülow's wife, Sunny, and his stepson, Alexander von Auersperg, later claimed that they were all lies and that he had been paid by von Bülow for his part in the deception. Furthermore, Marriott had secretly tape-recorded conversations with Father Magaldi, von Bülow, and Andrea Reynolds to attempt to support his claim. On one tape that I listened to, Father Magaldi and Marriott discuss von Bülow's alleged offer to help the priest be elevated to bishop. On another there is talk about getting the late Raymond Patriarca, the Mafia chieftain of Providence, to get a drug dealer serving time in jail to say that Alexander von Auersperg had been one of his customers.

This murky matter played no part in Claus von Bülow's second trial in Providence. However, there were frequent rumors that Father Magaldi, who is a popular priest in the city, was about to be indicted for lying in a sworn statement he had given in 1983 to help von Bülow get a new trial, and that may have been the principal reason why Judge Corinne Grande insisted that the jury be sequestered for the eight weeks of the trial, especially since several of the members were acquainted with Father Magaldi. The priest was not indicted until after the jury had retired to deliberate, and the contents of the sealed indictment were not made known.

On the day before the jury returned its verdict, Claus von Bülow and Father Magaldi met—perhaps by accident, perhaps by design—in the lobby of the Biltmore Plaza Hotel.

The encounter took place at seven o'clock on a Sunday morning and was witnessed by one of the bellmen, who used to
serve as an altar boy for Father Magaldi. The priest, the
bellman told me, had made the fifteen-minute drive from
North Providence to buy the Sunday papers at the newsstand
in the lobby of the hotel. Just as he arrived, the elevator doors
opened and von Bülow emerged to walk Mrs. Reynolds's
golden retriever, Tiger Lily. The encounter between the two
men was brief, but the bellman was sure they had exchanged
a few words.

That night, twelve members of the media who had covered
the trial gathered for a farewell dinner in a Providence restaurant. Their conversation never strayed far from the subject
that had held them together for nearly nine weeks—the trial.
They discussed the fact that once again Claus von Bülow had
not taken the stand, and they felt that it had been a foregone
conclusion in the defense strategy from the start that he was
never going to. The defense was aware that the prosecution
was in possession of an exhaustive report by a European
private-detective agency on the life of von Bülow before
his marriage to Sunny, and a clever prosecutor, given the opportunity to examine the defendant directly, would have
been able to ask many potentially embarrassing questions.
Another topic of conversation was Judge Corinne Grande,
whose frequent rulings favorable to the defense raised questions of her impartiality. In what was certainly the most
controversial ruling of the trial, Judge Grande had agreed
with von Bülow's lawyers that the testimony of G. Morris
Gurley, Sunny's banker at the Chemical Bank in New York,
should be barred. Gurley would certainly have testified
that, according to a prenuptial agreement, von Bülow would
receive nothing from his wife in a divorce. However,
according to her will, he would inherit $14 million if she
died.

I repeated a story I had heard that afternoon from someone
who had been present at an exchange between Mr. Gurley
and Alexandra Isles in the witness room. Mrs. Isles had just

completed her testimony when Gurley was informed that he would not be called to the stand. Gurley was stunned. So was Mrs. Isles. "I can't believe they're not letting you testify," she told him. "I wasn't the motive, Morris. The money was the motive. He had me for free."

Late in the evening someone came up with the idea, since there were twelve of us, of pretending to be a jury and voting a verdict, not as we anticipated the jury would vote, but as we would vote if we were members of the jury and knew everything we knew rather than what Judge Grande had selected for us to know. The waitress brought a pad and pencils, and each person cast his vote. Our verdict, we all agreed, would remain our secret.

During the four days the jury was out deliberating, Claus von Bülow wandered up and down the crowded corridors of the courthouse, chain-smoking Vantage cigarettes and behaving like a genial host at a liquorless cocktail party, moving from one group of reporters to another with his endless supply of anecdotes. He even took time to call his most consistently loyal friend, the art historian John Richardson, to ask when he planned to leave for London. Monday week, he was told. He asked Richardson if he would take twelve large bags of potato chips to Paul Getty, Jr., who loved potato chips, but only the American kind.

On Monday morning, June 10, 1985, while waiting for the jury to reappear, von Bülow was tense and withdrawn. In the minutes before the jury entered, Barbara Nevins, a popular CBS reporter, leaned over from the press box and asked him if he had any final words before the verdict was delivered. In an uncharacteristic gesture, von Bülow raised the middle finger of his left hand to her.

"Is that for me, Mr. von Bülow, or for the press in general?" asked Miss Nevins. Thinking better of his gesture, he pretended that he had meant to scratch his forehead. At that moment the jury entered.

The proceedings were swift. The verdict was, predictably,

"Not Guilty" on both charges. Von Bülow bowed his head for an instant and blinked back a tear. Then he and his lawyer Thomas Puccio nodded to each other without emotion. The courtroom was strangely mute despite a few cheers from elderly Clausettes in the back of the room. Very little of the ecstasy that accompanies a vindication was present, except in the histrionics of Mrs. Reynolds, whose moment had finally come, and she played it to the hilt. Flanked by two of her favorite reporters and directly in line with the television camera, she raised her diamond-ringed fingers to her diamond-earringed ears and wept.

In his moment of victory, von Bülow bypassed the embrace and kiss offered him by Mrs. Reynolds, who was wearing the same blue party dress she had worn at her granddaughter's christening, and gave her a peck on the cheek. Then he raced to a telephone to call Cosima.

During the triumphant press conference after the trial, von Bülow, surrounded by seven lawyers glowing with the flush of victory, returned to his old arrogance as he fielded questions from media representatives he no longer needed to court. Following a champagne visit with the jury that had acquitted him, he and Mrs. Reynolds returned to New York. Even in his moment of victory, dramatic rumors preceded his arrival. At Mortimer's restaurant, a French visitor said that if Claus had been found guilty, there was a plan to spirit him out of the country on the private jet of a vastly rich Texan.

"If I took you down to our beach and you started asking people, the two hundred of us who have dinner and swim and play golf together, you would find nearly everybody will say he did it," Mrs. John Slocum, a member of Newport society whose pedigree goes back twelve generations, told a reporter a week before von Bülow was acquitted. "And I'll tell you something else," she added, "people are afraid of Claus."

A few days after the trial, I went to Newport to check out the scene, and found that the battle lines between the pro- and anti-von Bülow factions remained drawn, and seemed

possibly even fiercer than ever. On the front page of the
Newport Daily News, Mrs. Slocum crossed swords with Mrs.
John Nicholas Brown, who had been von Bülow's staunchest
defender in Newport society from the beginning, in their
respective damnation and praise of Judge Grande and the
verdict. In the same article Mrs. Claiborne Pell, the wife of
Senator Pell of Rhode Island, said she was "delighted" that
von Bülow had walked from the courthouse a free man, while
Hugh D. Auchincloss, the stepbrother of Jacqueline Kennedy
Onassis, who had once written a letter in von Bülow's behalf
to help him gain membership in the Knickerbocker Club, had
harsh words for the verdict, the judge, and his former friend.

At the exclusive Clambake Club, Russell Aitken, the wid-
ower of Sunny von Bülow's mother, Annie-Laurie Aitken,
stared ahead stone-faced as Mr. and Mrs. John Winslow, who
had once said that the Aitkens would not be welcome at
Bailey's Beach if Claus were acquitted, were seated nearby
with their party. The Winslows were equally stone-faced.

Russell Aitken's dislike of his stepson-in-law is ferocious, and
it predates the two charges of attempted murder by insulin
injection. Standing on the terrace of Champs Soleil, the
Bellevue Avenue estate he inherited from his late wife, which
rivals, perhaps even surpasses, Clarendon Court in splendor,
Mr. Aitken recalled for me the first time he and his wife ever
met Claus von Bülow. It was in 1966 in London, in the
lounge of Claridge's hotel, when von Bülow was a suitor for
Sunny, who had just divorced Prince Alfie von Auersperg.
Von Bülow arrived for the meeting with Sunny's parents with
his head covered in bandages, explaining that he had been in
an automobile accident. Later Mr. and Mrs. Aitken heard
from Sunny that the truth was rather different: his head was
bandaged because he had just had his first hair-transplant
operation.

Behind Russell Aitken, on the rolling lawns of the French
manor house, a new croquet court was under construction,
which promises to be the handsomest croquet court on the

Eastern Seaboard. A respected sculptor, he had had one of his own artworks installed on a wall overlooking the new court. Mr. Aitken interrupted his tour to continue our con-versation about his stepson-in-law. "He is an extremely dan-gerous man," he said, "because he's a Cambridge-educated con man with legal training. He is totally amoral, greedy as a wolverine, cold-blooded as a snake. And I apologize to the snake."

"May I quote you saying that, Mr. Aitken?" I asked.

"Oh, yes, indeed," he replied.

While von Bülow saved himself for an exclusive interview with Barbara Walters on "20/20," his mistress did a saturation booking on the television shows. Back in Providence, Judge Grande defended herself against a barrage of criticism that she had let a guilty man walk free. "I DIDN'T HELP CLAUS BEAT RAP," went one headline. Out in Seattle, Jennie Bülow, the elderly widow of Frits Bülow, Claus von Bülow's long-dead maternal grandfather, from whom he acquired his name when he changed it from Borberg, made no secret of her dissatisfaction with both the judge and the verdict.

In New York, von Bülow announced that he would visit Sunny at Columbia-Presbyterian Medical Center for the first time in four years as a gesture of his continuing love for her. Later, seated in the library of his wife's Fifth Avenue apart-ment, he met with Barbara Walters, as he had met with her at the conclusion of his first trial. He talked about his desire to go back to work. "I was never going to divorce Sunny because of any other woman," he told her. "I was going to divorce Sunny because she didn't tolerate my work." At the end of the interview, Miss Walters announced that von Bülow would soon be leaving for England to begin work for Paul Getty, Jr., the son of his former boss.

Getty, who was very possibly the donor of both von Bülow's bail money and his defense fund, is fifty-two years old and makes his home in England. He recently gave $63 million to the National Gallery in London. In 1984, according to *For-*

tune magazine, he had an income from the Getty trust of $110 million. A virtual recluse, Getty is said to be a registered drug addict in England. His second wife, Talitha Pol, a popular member of the jet set, died in her husband's penthouse apartment in Rome of a massive overdose of heroin in 1971. To this day many of her friends insist that the fatal injection was not self-administered. The oldest of Getty's five children, John Paul III, lost an ear during his kidnapping in Italy in 1973. He later suffered a methadone-induced stroke that left him blind and crippled. Getty's youngest child, Tara Gabriel Galaxy Gramaphone Getty, seventeen, the son of Talitha, is at present engaged in legal proceedings against the $4 billion Getty trust.

In the ongoing controversy that constantly surrounds him, von Bülow for some reason denied to reporter Ellen Fleysher during a news conference an item in Liz Smith's syndicated column saying that he and Mrs. Reynolds had posed for *Vanity Fair* magazine and photographer Helmut Newton dressed in black leather. "No, I think you've got the wrong case," he told the reporter. Liz Smith, quick to respond, printed in her column two days later, "Once you see Claus inside the magazine in his black leather jacket, I want you to tell me how we can believe anything he says."

The same day that Liz Smith questioned von Bülow's veracity, the *New York Times* reported that the indictment against Father Magaldi in Providence had been unsealed and that the priest was charged with perjury and conspiring to obstruct justice to affect the outcome of Claus von Bülow's appeal. Early that morning the telephone rang in my New York apartment. It was Mrs. Reynolds. Displeased with the latest developments in the media, she accused me of planting the story in Liz Smith's column to attract publicity for my article in *Vanity Fair*.

"Do you have any fear of being subpoenaed in the Father Magaldi case?" I asked her.

"They wouldn't subpoena me over their dead bodies," replied Mrs. Reynolds.

"Why?"

"I can totally demolish Mr. Marriott," she said. There was ice in her voice.

I asked her if it was true that she and von Bülow were only waiting for the return of his passport so that they could get out of the country before they were subpoenaed. She angrily denied to me that they had played any part in the false affidavits.

Von Bülow now got on the line, and his anger equaled that of Mrs. Reynolds. "I suggest you talk with Professor Dershowitz at Harvard," he told me sternly.

"Let me give you his telephone number," snapped Mrs. Reynolds, "to save you the seventy-five cents it will cost you to dial information."

The burning question was, would Claus von Bülow's acquittal give him automatic use of his comatose wife's $3.5 million annual income, minus, of course, the half-million dollars a year it costs to maintain her in Columbia-Presbyterian Medical Center? If so, his access to the money was not immediate, and civil litigation loomed that could tie up Sunny's fortune for years. In the meantime, unless Sunny dies and von Bülow inherits the $14 million that he is guaranteed in her will, he will have to make do with the interest on the $2 million trust his wife gave to the Metropolitan Opera, which amounts to $120,000 a year before taxes. There was talk in the first week of his freedom that money was tight.

Despite the wide coverage of von Bülow's acquittal across the country, the accolades of victory were spare in New York. The jewelry designer Kenneth Jay Lane entertained von Bülow and Mrs. Reynolds at a lunch in their honor—cold curried chicken, pasta salad, raspberries and blueberries with crème fraîche—and the guest list included John Richardson; Giorgio co-owner Gale Hayman; the English film star Rachel

Ward; her husband, Australian actor Bryan Brown; and her mother, Claire Ward, longtime companion of von Bülow's great friend Lord Lambton, a former parliamentary undersecretary for the Royal Air Force who was forced to resign after his involvement in a government sex scandal. The lunch coincided with the announcement in the *New York Times* of Father Magaldi's indictment, and one guest reported that the atmosphere was subdued.

While von Bülow waited for his passport to be returned, he and Mrs. Reynolds became—for them, at least—almost socially invisible. They lunched quietly at Le Cirque, with their staunch ally Alice Mason, the New York realtor and hostess. On another occasion Mrs. Reynolds entertained two members of the press at lunch at the Four Seasons. They attended a coming-out party given in honor of two daughters of the family with whom Cosima had lived during the first trial. For some reason they did not once venture into Mortimer's, the Upper East Side restaurant that had become their favorite haunt between trials.

Mrs. Reynolds told friends she was writing a miniseries based on the trial. Von Bülow made plans with his publisher for his autobiography and according to one friend, made arrangements for a face-lift. Together they visited the Livingston Manor house of Mrs. Reynolds's about-to-be-former husband, Sheldon Reynolds, to look at trees she had planted and pick up clothes she had left there. A witness to the scene reported that von Bülow's attitude to Mrs. Reynolds was chilly.

Alexandra Isles declined to be interviewed at the end of the trial. "We all have our own ways of surviving," she wrote me. "Mine is to try to put it out of my head and get on with other things. I know you will understand that an interview somehow keeps it all 'unfinished business,' but here is a bit of irony you are welcome to use: It was my father who, in the Danish underground, got little Claus Borberg (in his boy scout uniform!) out of Denmark."

• • •

The participants began to scatter. Maria Schrallhammer, after twenty-eight years of service with Sunny Crawford von Auersperg von Bülow and her children, retired and returned to Germany the day after the verdict. Cosima von Bülow, eighteen, threw herself into the hectic whirl of a summer of debutante parties. Alexander von Auersperg returned to his job in the retirement division of E. F. Hutton. Ala Kneissl, pregnant with her second child, began work on a documentary film about victims of homicide. Together Ala and Alexander, through the Chemical Bank, which handles the fortunes of their mother and grandmother, are in the process of establishing two major foundations. One will provide funds for the solace of the families of homicide victims and for changes in legislation to allow victims' rights to equate with the rights of criminals. A second foundation, commemorating both their parents, will be for medical research in the field of comas. G. Morris Gurley, the bank officer who was not allowed to testify at the trial, is in charge of overseeing the foundations.

Von Bülow did not visit his wife at Columbia-Presbyterian Medical Center. Two weeks after the acquittal, his passport was returned to him, and for the first time in five years he was free to travel abroad. The next day he and Mrs. Reynolds left New York. They did not fly first class. He stopped in London to visit friends. Mrs. Reynolds, after a one-day stopover in London, went on to Geneva to visit her father. A few days later they rendezvoused at the Grand Hotel & de la Pace in the Italian spa of Montecatini Terme.

The third act of the von Bülow affair is still to be played. Will Father Magaldi be tried for lying in a sworn statement he gave to help von Bülow get a new trial? Will David Marriott, who once said and later recanted that he had delivered drugs, needles, and a hypodermic syringe to Clarendon Court, testify against his former friend and benefactor? Will Claus von Bülow and Mrs. Reynolds be called to testify at Father Magaldi's trial? Will the relationship of von Bülow and Mrs.

Reynolds sustain the serenity of his acquittal, with or without Sunny's income of $3.5 million a year? Will New York and London society receive the couple back into the charmed circle at the top?

The drama seems a long way from the final curtain, although Claus von Bülow's dark and spacious place in social history has been assured.